GOLD FROM THE FIRE

MAXINE HANCOCK

GOLD FROM THE FIRE

Postcards from a Prairie Pilgrimage

REGENT COLLEGE PUBLISHING
Vancouver, British Columbia

Published 2004 by
Regent College Publishing
5800 University Boulevard, Vancouver, BC V6T 2E4 Canada
www.regentpublishing.com

The essays collected here appeared in slightly different
form in *Faith Today* magazine of the
Evangelical Fellowship of Canada, 1990-1996.

Views expressed in works published by Regent College Publishing
are those of the authors and do not necessarily represent the official
position of Regent College <www.regent-college.edu>.

Unless otherwise noted, all Scripture quotations are from the
New International Version of the Bible.
Copyright © 1973, 1978 by the International Bible Society.
Used by permission of Zondervan Publishers.

Library and Archives Canada Cataloguing in Publication Data

Hancock, Maxine
Gold from the fire / Maxine Hancock.

ISBN 1-57383-233-2

1. Spirituality. 2. Faith. I. Title.

BL624.H36 2004   204   C2004-903869-9

CONTENTS

PREFACE

This is a gathering of essays written over a span of several years, presented as a collection of "postcards from a prairie pilgrimage."

I live in a rainforest now—in a grey-green abundantly watered world. But my faith was forged in a very different environment. Until recently I lived on the Canadian prairies that stretch, vast and golden, east of the Rocky Mountains. There, skies are huge and ever-changing, winters are long and often severe, and the devastating possibility of drought is never far from our minds. I grew up in Alberta cities: Lethbridge, Calgary, Edmonton. Then, when we were newly married, Cam and I went out to teach in the lovely parkland at the Alberta-Saskatchewan border half-way between Edmonton and Saskatoon, and didn't come back to city living until twenty-five years later when I returned to the University of Alberta, first to study and then to teach, and then on to Vancouver where I now teach at Regent College. We continued to farm for another ten years during these transitions; in our thirty-eight years of sowing and reaping, we learned together what it was to be up against the rocky bosom of God.

In those years, I planted gardens and wrote books while Cam planted and harvested grain crops; together we nurtured children--both those born of our flesh and those born of the Spirit. We were intimately linked to the landscape, to church and community, to the earth. What affected any of these affected us: when it went well for the land, it went well for us; when the land cried out for rain, our very spirits thirsted, our whole beings cried out. And in all of that, we learned to know a God who does not exist for our sake, but we for his.

And there was, as promised, sufficiency. Every crop harvested was a material evidence of God's providence; when the crops faltered, we learned in new ways the truth, "My grace is sufficient." Sufficiency in either case, in good times and bad.

The years during which I wrote these essays were difficult ones in many ways. Our four children entered adult life, with all the crises and decisions that entails. Just as I completed doctoral studies, a son came back to the farm with two little daughters for whom he had been granted sole custody. The girls were toddlers—not yet two and just-turned four years old, and together with our son we worked to create a family cover of love and care to meet the needs of the little ones. My long-deferred entry into a world of scholarship and teaching, already postponed, was put on hold again for another season of waiting, as I learned again the tender heart of One who loved, and loves still the little children, and all that is small or vulnerable or undervalued.

As these things happened, our area of the prairies also endured a prolonged dry period that lasted with growing intensity for, finally, about fifteen years. Cam had changed his farming practices from conventional methods to zero-tillage in order to conserve diminishing moisture. But with each year scanting us even further, growing crops became increasingly challenging. So the backdrop to these essays is often stress. But what was always there, attested to by Scripture, borne witness to by the love within a village church, was the steadfast love of a caring God.

The rains have come again to our beloved farm land in Alberta; while we no longer actually farm the land, we still care deeply about its well-being. Our little village church has gone on baptizing new believers every year, and continues to bear its remarkable witness of love in the community. Our son is happily remarried. And, here in Vancouver, we are now very well-watered. But what we learned in the prairie years is written in our hearts; these essays are short readings from long lessons.

One always accumulates debts in bringing a book into being. My thanks to Audrey Dorsch, editor-in-chief of *Faith Today* where these pieces first saw publication; to Karen Hollenbrook Wuest who edited the columns into book form, thoughtfully grouping the essays into the book's four sections. My thanks, too, to Rob Clements of Regent College Publishing; to Bill Reimer, Regent College Bookstore Manager; and to Dal Schindell, Director of Publications, Regent College. Their creative collaboration enriches all us at Regent College: thank you, my friends. To the Awards Committee of the Canadian Church Press Association who named my signed column "Best Column" (1997)—I am thankful for the encouragement that these essays might be worth collecting and sharing with another audience. And as always, my thanks to Cam: whatever would I do or be without him?

Maxine Hancock
Regent College, Vancouver BC
Fall, 2004

LIVING ON THE STRETCH

Reflections on Hospitality & Community

1

LIVING ON THE STRETCH

Enlarge the place of your tent,
stretch your tent curtains wide,
do not hold back;
lengthen your cords,
strengthen your stakes.

ISAIAH 54:1-2

There's a wonderful word picture in Isaiah 54 of God's people as a desert woman: "Sing . . . Do not be afraid . . . For your Maker is your husband" (v. 5). I suppose I have personally related to this image during various desert times in my life: during the dry stretches of illness, during times when financial hardship scorched away joy, during barren times when church conflict seared my spirit, or when I returned to academic study some years ago and felt like I was pitching my little tent in a world of arid intellectualism, seeking a stream of joy in a wasteland of competing ideas.

If I often have felt like a desert woman personally, we as God's people collectively answer the description even more fully. In the moral wasteland of our society, survival of anything spiritual is continuously threatened. Being God's people in a post-modern age means learning to live tenaciously.

Yet the word picture in Isaiah 54 encourages God's desert people to "enlarge the place of your tent, stretch your tent curtains wide." It invites us to "live on the stretch"—openly, abundantly, joyfully—in the midst of our desert surroundings.

The tent needs to be enlarged because the apparently deserted wife is to be fruitful, to bear children. Fruitfulness in the spiritual sense has a dual significance: the bearing of spiritual children, bringing people to new life in Christ; and the bearing of the "fruit of the Spirit," developing holiness in life. Both kinds of fruitfulness require a people of God who are willing to live on the stretch, to enter into the glad pain of travail for the birth of others, to open our tent curtains wide in hospitality to the Spirit of God.

This "expanding tent" metaphor also suggests an attitude of abundance, of living richly. In the desert, the more tent poles a tent has, the richer its owner is known to be. Although Jesus said very clearly that he had come "that we might have life, and have it more abundantly" (John 10:10), the narrow, cramped lives of many "one-pole" Christians suggest the opposite.

Of course, I am not talking about a "success gospel," about becoming rich and famous because we love Jesus. I am talking about living in the fullness of God's provision, which the New Testament tells us God has "laid by" in Christ. When we are living in union with Christ, we have in and through him "all things that pertain to life and godliness" (2 Pet 1:3).

We are, as God's people, the desert wife of a very rich sheik. And we are invited to "show off" his goodness to us by living abundantly, largely, experiencing his grace as it touches every area of life and extending that grace to others.

And that's another part of this "desert woman" image of an enlarged and enlarging tent: we are called to live hospitably, with our lives opened out to others rather than closed down and zipped up. As Christians, we tend to set up neat little tents around a discovered oasis and then live closed off to everyone else. We become busy with church programs, busy in sharing our lives with others who share our assumptions about life.

But desert hospitality is legendary and, indeed, essential to survival. In fact, as Dr. Helen Huston, a medical missionary to Nepal, told a University of Alberta convocation, at which she received an honorary doctorate, "The greatest crime in the desert is knowing where there is water and not telling another." We claim to have found the living water, to have our desert tents pitched beside it. And when we are depicted as God's desert people, living as strangers and pilgrims in an alien and hostile environment, we are at the same time being invited to live openly, hospitably, inviting others to share in the plenty we have discovered.

Living expansively means being open to the wayfarers who will encounter our tents, being unafraid to interact with them and their ideas, willing and glad to share our abundance with them. And this image is also the sign of a sojourning people, who pitch their fragile, vulnerable and portable tents here only for a little before moving on.

We live in a parched and desert society that does not nurture grace. But we are, as God's people, the desert wife of a great king, and our expansive, open, hospitable lifestyles should provide a shelter in that desert for others and a home for those who are born into the desert family.

It will keep all of us living on the spiritual and intellectual stretch to live out the implications of this picture of the church. And if we, as God's people (collectively or individually), are going to live more openly, more expansively, we will need to "lengthen the cords" of our trust and "strengthen the stakes" of our knowledge of God (Isa 54:2). Because, of course, we wouldn't want to have our desert tent turn into a kite—and some dry, hot day of wind and sand, just blow away.

2

COLD WELCOME

He was in the world, and though the world was made through him, the world did not recognize him. He came to that which was his own, but his own did not receive him. Yet to all who received him, to those who believed in his name, he gave the right to become children of God.

JOHN 1:10-12

Sometimes, when I'm standing waiting for her to come to answer the doorbell," a friend once told me, "I look at the door, and I remember that Christmas Eve." And he went on to tell me about that winter night when the door that now opens wide for him had been literally closed in his face.

Christmas, with its goodwill and general warm feelings, had seemed a time to try once more to mend his broken relationship with the people who lived behind that door. Somehow, it didn't seem right—didn't even seem possible—that these people, who all named Jesus as Lord, should be shutting each other out of their lives, locked in misunderstanding and unforgiveness.

Perhaps, he thought, if he arrived at the door with some gifts, he would be received along with the tokens of his desire to forgive—and to be forgiven. So he made up his parcel of carefully chosen and festively wrapped gifts and, full of both hope and trepidation, went to that door. He pressed the doorbell and stood, waiting.

When at last the lady of the house came to the door and saw him, she opened the door wide enough to exchange a few civil greetings, received the gifts—and shut the door. He stood outside in the December cold, now made suddenly more bitter. What made it especially hard was that the woman who shut her door against him was his mother.

That experience—though long past—helps my friend feel the jolt that the apostle John must have intended when he wrote, "[Jesus] came unto his own, and his own received him not" (John 1:11).

To come, but not to be received or invited in, is a particularly painful experience. To have someone accept the gift you bring but fail to welcome you as the giver of that gift is perhaps even more painful. And yet that is just what happened when Jesus came into this world, which he created.

And it is what happens again, year after year, as the world prepares for Christmas. Each Christmas season, I am amazed at how much joy and love spills over into the world because of Jesus' coming—even though he has been overwhelmingly rejected as Lord. Still the bells ring; still the songs are sung; still food pours into the food banks and people volunteer to wrap donated gifts for children. Jesus' gifts are welcomed once again.

And if one could possibly trace all the art, all the music, all the agencies of caring and learning that exist throughout the world because of Jesus, the list of gifts we have eagerly reached out to receive would become very long indeed.

But what about the giver? What about the hands that hold out the gifts of redemptive love to our society? Our society still accepts the gifts Jesus brings but shuts the door against him personally.

It was a cold welcome for the Word-became-flesh then, and it is a cold welcome he's offered yet. Fortunately, though, John does not end his story with the rejected gift-giver. There were some then, as there are a some now, who welcome the gift-giver as well as the gifts, and in their acceptance of the one who is God-come-to-us, they receive that gift beyond all others: "power to become the children of God"—inclusion in the family of believers.

The door that once was shut against my friend is open to him again now in fellowship, a witness to the power of love to heal and restore broken human relationships.

But my friend still remembers that cold Christmas Eve and that cold welcome. And because of his story, I will continue to ask myself if we, in all of our Christmas cheer and festivities, have seized the gifts of love and joy that Christ bears, but have left him standing outside in the bitter cold.

> O Jesus, Thou art standing
> Outside the fast-closed door,
> In lowly patience waiting
> To pass the threshold o'er.
> Shame on us, Christian brothers,
> His Name and sign who bear,
> O shame, thrice shame upon us,
> To keep him standing there.
>
> —William How

3

ALONGSIDING

As they talked and discussed these things with each other,
Jesus himself came up and walked along with them.

LUKE 24:15

In our family we had brave kids and timid kids. Heather, who is now a speech pathologist in Chicago, was a timid one. So sending her by Greyhound Bus from the farm to her grandparents in the city when she was nine or ten was traumatic—for her and for me. She was being brave, but getting quieter and paler and holding my hand tighter and tighter as the time came to step onto the bus.

Then we heard a familiar voice behind us. "Are you traveling my way, Heather?" We turned to see the wife of a cousin of ours, her face reflecting kindness and reassurance. Suddenly the whole trip was changed. Heather was not going to have to travel alone. Someone had come alongside to share her journey with her.

"Alongsiding" has been a special privilege in my life. Again and again I have felt the honour of others letting me share some particularly difficult part of their journey—not because I had great wisdom or great strength or great anything, just because

I was there and was willing to walk with them for a stretch of the journey.

A young neighbour, beside herself with grief over her toddler's accidental drowning, needing someone to help her read the map of an unknown and terrifying terrain.

A middle-aged woman coping with the shock of learning that her husband was unfaithful to the marriage she had thought was strong enough to build her life on.

A bewildered young city woman married to a neighbour in our farming community needing help to "read the codes" of a different culture.

A graduate student struggling with a thesis needing someone to listen while he worked out the complex ideas he wanted to pin down on paper.

A young mother battling fatigue and wondering if she would ever again be the person she was before babies.

A couple wondering if the effort of building their battered marriage was really worth it.

My job has been to listen, to enter into each person's room of grief or perplexity or darkness and to sit with them there—and then to walk with them towards the light. And when the way has become nearly too hard for them to go on, to climb a little knoll and survey the countryside ahead and say, "I think we can get through here," or "The road gets better again just after this."

It takes time to be an alongsider, of course.

I remember the winter I served as an alongsider to a neighbour wrapped in the grave-clothes of a long depression. As to Lazarus, Jesus had spoken the word of new life to her; as to his disciples, he spoke the command to me: "Take off the grave clothes and let her go." One morning as I was making the bed, eager to get to my desk and write, the phone rang. The Lord asked me pointedly, "Are you willing to give me the time it will take to set this woman free?"

Over the next months my friend and I spent hours together—walking, studying the Scriptures, baking, laughing, talking and sharing.

She became an effective communicator of the gospel to others in the community and a very dear personal friend. The gift of time was multiplied back to me in many ways, and today my friend walks in light and life.

And, for me, there have been others who have come alongside me just when I needed to know that I was not abandoned. There was a young pastor who put his head down on his arms and wept with us many years ago as a cattle-feeding partnership we had formed failed and folded. His loving care was part of what gave us the strength to rebuild.

A neighbour woman, several years younger than I, called on me after the community newspaper had published word of my brother's death. "I read that you lost your brother," she said. "Most people don't realize how hard that can be—but I lost a brother, too, about three years ago. And I know it's very hard." Like a ministering angel, she came alongside me and walked with me in my summer of grief.

There have been fellow-scholars who understood the stress of graduate studies.

And there was a wonderful group of young adults who joined me for an evening a week to discuss how best we might use today's opportunities to communicate the gospel—grappling with the hard questions that we have to consider if we are going to get the good news out.

Alongsiders, all—and how grateful I am for them.

Of all the resurrection stories, my favourite is the story of the walk on the road to Emmaus when, as the grieving, puzzled disciples walked along, talking over the events of the death of their Lord, "Jesus himself came up and walked along with them" (Luke 24: 15).

Coming alongside each other to share the journey is one of the most effective ways we can bear witness to the risen Christ. Unchanging and fully faithful to his promise to be with us always, he is still Emmanuel: by his Spirit, in the Word, and in each other, God with us.

4

MAIL AT THE
END OF THE ROAD

*In the past God spoke to our forefathers through the prophets
at many times and in various ways, but in these last days he
has spoken to us by his Son, whom he appointed heir of all
things, and through whom he made the universe.*

HEBREWS 1:1-2

Do you still get your mail at the end of the road?"
the nostalgic letter writer asks in Rita MacNeil's song
"Shining Strong." MacNeil's voice pours, sweet and thick as
warmed honey, into my living room filled with winter light and
the gentle warmth of the wood fire in the cast-iron stove.

I find myself humming in answer, "No, I don't get my mail
at the end of the lane. We drive into town every other day or
so." Actually, the irregularity of occasional mail pick-up drives
me mildly crazy. Of course, with fax, phone and e-mail in the
electronic cottage our farm home has become, I can't exactly
complain of being cut off.

But one winter, long ago, I did get my mail at the end of a
long, snowy lane, and as I listen to the song, the memory is
suddenly strong in me. I was a young mother with four small

24

children under six, our family crammed into a tiny farmhouse set well back from the road on a little height of land from which, when the windows weren't curtained with a white lace of frost, we could see the whole sweep of the wide, shallow valley that stretched down and away from us, the nearest village a toy town halfway to the horizon. But in the winter I rarely saw the landscape, my world being the endless clutter of kids and toys in small spaces.

I was just beginning to write for publication and had discovered the sweet exaltations and sad disappointments of a freelance writer's mail. I would mail things out and wait, perhaps three or four weeks, before beginning to yearn for the letter that would bring me a word of acceptance. And it did not hurt to dream that maybe, sometime, the mail would bring me a cheque. By the time the self-addressed stamped envelope I never wanted to see again would arrive, bearing a returned manuscript, I had spent that cheque a dozen ways. But as time went on—and sometimes articles were accepted, and sometimes there were cheques and even letters from editors or copies of material that had just been published—I became increasingly addicted to mail.

For me, mail meant there was an outside world—people who, although they existed for me only as names, with unimaginable faces and indecipherable personalities, actually read my work and had the power to see it into print. For me, mail meant I was not alone or forgotten.

When we moved from the village, where I could walk downtown for my mail every day, to the farm, where I could not, I felt as though I would suffocate in the isolation. Cam was teaching in a town in the opposite direction from where we got our mail. I simply could not pack up four small children and put them in our not-so-dependable car and drive to town every day. It would have been far too costly in time, expense and—given our Alberta winters then—risk.

One Sunday a neighbour, who drove the school bus down our road, overheard me lament my lack of regular mail. She moved into the circle of the conversation I was having with another friend and said, "If you would get Cam to put a mailbox at the end of your lane and trust me with your mail key, I would pick up your mail when I get mine and drop it off for you on my way past."

Trust her with my mail key? I would have trusted her with my life in exchange for my mail. Cam built a mailbox, and for the rest of that long winter, I was able to walk to the end of our lane, often with tears of exhaustion or frustration freezing on my cheeks, pick up my mail and walk back. I was always refreshed by a few minutes of prayerful quiet, by the fresh air and exercise, and I was restored by the sense that there was still an outside world.

So much has changed since then. We moved to another site before building our own farm home. It is on another side of the same great valley I used to look across. We spend our winters in that "outside world" I used to only know by faith—and mail. The tumble of little children around my feet has resolved into the distant voices of grown children. But my need for a "word from outside" is as great as ever. My greeting to whichever family member who returns from town is still, "Did you get the mail?"

Perhaps my hunger for contact is more than the hunger of a city woman turned country wife for reassurance that there is a world bigger than farm and village. Perhaps it reflects the hunger of my spirit for a word from outside—outside my own sphere of existence, outside my own limited perspective, outside the clutter of my own preoccupations—a word that tells me there is more than I now can see or know, a word that names for me the one who created me and who calls me into communion, a word that tells me I am known and valued.

This is the word that God has spoken through his prophets and in his son, our Lord and Saviour, Jesus Christ. This is the word I hunger to receive from outside again and again and again.

5

AN OPEN HOME

"Anyone who loves his father or mother more than me is not worthy of me; anyone who loves his son or daughter more than me is not worthy of me; and anyone who does not take his cross and follow me is not worthy of me."

MATTHEW 10:37-38

Because everything human seems to swing between extremes, I both welcome and fear the new emphasis on family in our culture. I welcome it, of course, because it is about time that we recognize the significance of sound families to a healthy society.

But I fear that if our concern for family is not kept within the conditioning context of Christ's absolute claims on our devotion, we will simply exchange the current controlling idolatry of self-ism for the deceptive idolatry of family.

The enemy does a fine job of subverting all of God's good gifts, among which I count family one of the greatest: what he cannot convince us to despise and treat with contempt he entices us to worship. Such idolatry occurs when the good of an individual family is seen as the "be-all" and "end-all" of human existence and when the energies of the family are tied up in meeting its own needs.

As Rodney Clapp puts it in his excellent book, *Families at the Crossroads* (InterVarsity Press, 1993), "Family needs purpose beyond itself and its sentimentality to survive and prosper." Worship of the family, like any other idolatry, will cheat and finally enslave us.

God's people are called to place love for God at the very centre of existence; love for neighbour flows out from that (Mark 12:28–34). In this framework, family members are our nearest neighbours, to whom love and compassionate care are due. Many families today are learning how to re-extend themselves to include several generations—an ancient idea, but revolutionary in a day of individualization and fragmentation.

But when we have been good only to those who love or belong to us, Jesus makes it clear that we have done nothing more than pagans who do not acknowledge God. In the kingdom of God we are called out of our families of origin and marriage ties into a new family, the people of God; out of kin into a new connection as "a chosen people, a royal priesthood, a holy nation, a people belonging to God" (1 Pet 2:9–10). Although in recent years cults have debased the image of the church as family, they merely counterfeit the genuine relationship that Jesus announced upon his resurrection, a new family birthed in a new relationship to God (John 20:17).

It was the genius of the early church that it grasped the truth and wonder of this relationship. It was as family that the church survived four centuries of persecution; as family it will be able to survive until Jesus returns in glad reunion with it.

The healthiest and happiest of Christian families find a balance between meeting each other's needs within the immediate and extended family and being attentive to the needs of others in the local and global church and in the human community outside of the church.

Hospitality is one obvious opportunity for the outflow of family love to others; the inclusion of other than kin at every family time of celebration might well be considered part of making that celebration Christian. And hospitality goes beyond "one-shot" dinner invitations. It means opening the family to the participation of others. If all Christian families included one or more single people or single-parent families or lonely, insecure teenagers as part of their family circle, the church as family would come much closer to being realized.

An open home allows for the unstaged mentoring of new family units as people watch and interact with real people in the reality of everyday family life. Courteous interactions, conflict resolution and all the gritty reality of people living together are better learned in the action of family living than in the best-run seminars on family life.

Many families are growing together by physically serving the needs of others within their own communities by working together in a food bank or forging a family connection with a needy family. And some families are helping their children gain an international perspective by building connections with missionaries—exchanging letters, becoming prayer partners or visiting the mission or project. Such connections stimulate us to recognize that we are part of a global family of which the North American branch is a materially rich but in many other ways impoverished member.

The family exists for far more than itself. It can realize itself only by losing itself in the larger whole, the family that is the church. Only as it is connected to something bigger than itself will the family really help its members move beyond selfishness.

Our society needs homes that view themselves as "service centres," places where people are welcomed and accepted, where ministry is envisioned and enacted as a family activity. As husbands, wives and children serve together, they are forged into a unit of evangelism, witness and service. This can strengthen their own commitments to one another, and it will certainly challenge the "we four and no more" spirit of today's cocooning urge.

Like all other social trends, the return to an emphasis on family needs to be held up to the searching critique of the gospel so that we can respond to it in a distinctively Christian way.

6

FREE AS WILD FRUIT

Greater love has no one than this, that he lay down his life for his friends. You are my friends if you do what I command. I no longer call you servants, because a servant does not know his master's business. Instead, I have called you friends. . . .

JOHN 15:13-15

The flowering of our woodlots is a quiet, gracious spectacle, the pin-cherry bushes draped in fragile snow-white lace as tremulous as veiled girls awaiting First Communion, the saskatoon bushes with their sturdier creamy-white blossoms as fresh as milkmaids at a country fair. All of the flowering native fruit bushes together make clouds of white under the newly leafed poplars and maples. If the frost holds off and the rains come, we enjoy a good harvest of free, native fruit.

Some seasons are specially memorable, seasons when the pin-cherries swing in the breeze on their slender threads like beaded earrings, and the saskatoons are round and juicy, hanging like bunches of miniature grapes. Then the tall bushes take two to pick—one to hold down the branches so the other can strip the ripe berries into the pail.

For me, friendship is like the wild, native fruit of our parkland. While family relationships are grown in the garden of my life, lovingly cultivated, carefully tended and richly productive, friendships have something fortuitous, free and freeing about them; they are a continual surprise of undeserved and undemanded beauty and generosity. Each friendship is a sign of grace.

I am richly blessed in friendships that cross the gaps between five generations, each friend giving life a special flavour. When I used to take a drive with my friend, May, then ninety-five, we would stop to view the rolling fertile green countryside from a height of land we both love. Long ago, she and her husband owned this land; others owned it before they did and after, and now our name is on it. She remembers picking berries here, and that there were once plum trees at the house site. We drive around to see if they are still there at the patch of uncultivated land that marks where a house and barn once stood, but only caraganas thrive there now.

She knows who homesteaded here—and over there and there and there. We sip tea, hot from the thermos, and chat about the beauty, the people who have come and gone. Because of my friendship with May, I find myself reflecting on what might be important to me when I am old. I look through the lens of her reflections to see what things ought to have priority now.

I have another special friendship that has long sustained me with a woman my mother's age who has an appetite for life and work and experience that daunts me and makes me feel pale and apathetic by comparison. Elsie keeps me looking forward to the next stage of life, helps me know that there are renewals of vitality after seasons of sorrow or sickness. Her sense of loss, unblunted by all the years, at having been deprived of an education by the Great Depression, reminds me that I am blessed among women in having had the privilege of study. Elsie has been alongside me all through my family years, a loyal and trustworthy friend of unending, undemanding kindness.

In my own generation, I value highly a number of soul-sisters who have shared with me the losses and challenges and changes of mid-life. Lorraine, Dorothy, Bonnie and I think through life together, pray and cry and laugh together, and our conversations serve as mirrors in which we can see ourselves reflected lovingly but truly back.

A generation down, I have friendships with a number of young women; some, like Donna, live within the farming community where we live, busy with family and growing gardens and taking meals to the fields; some, like Arlette, are part of the university community, busy juggling scholarly research and family duties. These young women keep me sharp, press insistent questions home to me, help me think about the dilemmas of life as they are facing them, where new options create new and complex conditions for ancient choices. I am blessed that they let me encourage them to reach out for life while maintaining commitments to God and their loved ones.

And another generation down from that, grandchildren open up new friendships. With these little ones I learn again the importance of story telling and have a chance to tell my old favourites—from Bible stories to fairy tales and fables to made-up-as-we-go yarns and rhymes. I marvel at how narrative shapes and secures our sense of reality, remembering again that God reveals himself to us not in theological abstraction or proposition but in a Great Story.

As free for the taking as the saskatoons and wild cherries, friendships across the generations sustain me with their gratuitous beauty and generosity. Though nothing is owed me, so much is given.

Jesus says, "I have called you friends" (John 15:15), and I realize that Jesus invites me into *friendship* with God, and I am overwhelmed with wild joy and gratitude.

God, the creator of the universe—and of the native fruit—offers himself to me in friendship, a friendship that spans not merely generations but all of time, a friendship that is all grace.

Jesus holds down for me the heavily fruited bough, and with my purple, juice-stained hands I take and eat.

ON THE
WINGS OF THE WIND

Reflections on Faith & Hope
Amidst Suffering and Trials

7

ON THE WINGS OF THE WIND

"Flesh gives birth to flesh, but the Spirit gives birth to spirit. You should not be surprised at my saying, 'You must be born again.' The wind blows wherever it pleases. You hear its sound, but you cannot tell where it comes from or where it is going. So it is with everyone born of the Spirit."

JOHN 3:6-8

Who has seen the wind?
  Neither you nor I:
But when the trees bow down their heads,
  The wind is passing by.
—*Christina Rosetti*

Learning Rosetti's poem as a child in Lethbridge I wanted to protest: "I have … well, I have *almost* seen the wind." Certainly, I had seen Chief Mountain distant and blue under a chinook arch. I had known days when we planned to go skating in the morning and in the afternoon needed rubber boots. I had spread my arms and let the wind send me running and dancing on my way, or had bowed my head and pushed against its power.

More recently, once when my husband and I drove from Banff to Calgary alongside an incoming chinook, I felt I was as close to seeing the wind as anyone could get. That day, a soft prism of colour with the faintest hues of pink, yellow and blue spread along the ragged edge of grey cloud that was the wing of the wind. Warm air from the Pacific swept over the mountains and down across the frozen Alberta countryside with winds reaching up to 100 kilometres per hour. We had left Calgary three days earlier, shivering in a -40°C deep freeze, and now were driving back into a city of slush and shirtsleeves, the temperature at 8°C and rising.

The warm wind rocked trees which hours earlier had stood stiffly at attention. In their suddenly supple branches, winter birds that for days had huddled in hiding now chirped and twittered. Over the stately blue and white march of the mountains, an arch of grey cloud curved over a pale turquoise blue sky.

For me, hope is a chinook arch and the wild, free joy of a wind that warms. No doubt this shapes my theology and my outlook on life as well. When you have lived in a place where chinook winds blow, you really do believe that anything can happen. You believe in the unexpected, in grace. You live ready for the exhilarating challenge of sudden change.

So when I get caught in a chinook, I feel a wonderful exhilaration. If the rainbow is the sign of God's covenant of faithfulness, the chinook arch is surely a sign of his grace.

When I get a chance again to walk in a chinook wind, as I do occasionally, I want to spread my arms and let the wind push me. I want to live in hope, aware of grace, ready for change, subject to the breath of God. I want to be aware of and responsive to the wind. I want to go with the wind—not against it. Walking against a chinook gale is exhausting; walking with it is exhilarating.

The chinook reminds us of the wonderful irregularities of grace. Within the regularities of the Noachic covenant (Gen 8:22) are many surprises. Within the new-every-morning faithfulness of God, there are frequent changes in the life of the believer—changes that seem to be designed to keep us moving forward in life, to remind us of our pilgrim status, to keep us from becoming complacent or from settling into predictable patterns in which we are no longer aware of our absolute dependence on God. People who have lived with the chinook can believe in change and welcome it; change is not viewed as a threat but as something to anticipate and enjoy.

When you live aware of a power that can alter an entire climate in a few short hours, you learn to live in hope. Though it may be -40°C today, with a chinook, it could be spring by tomorrow. Similarly, the most hopeless, locked-in or locked-up situation is not beyond God's power to change—and change dramatically. A God who can send chinooks can also change lives—and can thaw hearts, transform rigidly set habits, set rivers of joy running in frozen streets.

I am not, of course, the first to compare the "wind" with the "spirit." Jesus' words to Nicodemus make this link explicit: "You should not be surprised at my saying, 'You must be born again.' The wind blows wherever it pleases. You hear its sound, but you cannot tell where it comes from or where it is going. So it is with everyone born of the Spirit" (John 3:6–8). When Nicodemus heard these words, he would have related them to a very different experience of the wind from mine. But the very words of the Bible that are translated as "spirit" are words for the wind: *ru-ach* in Hebrew, *ru-cha* in Aramaic, and *pneuma* in Greek.

I have not quite seen the wind, but I have felt it, walked in it, lived in it. I want to keep living under the chinook arch of hope. I want the Spirit to thaw my winter heart, warm me, invigorate me. I want to know God's holy power to challenge the status quo.

Come, holy wind of God, over the mountains of our lives, I pray. Do not tiptoe or whisper, but roar, laugh, melt. Alter our plans. Breathe into us again the breath of life as a wind that is exhilarating, joyful and open to grace.

8

ENGRAVINGS

While [Jesus] was in Bethany, reclining at the table in the home of a man known as Simon the Leper, a woman came with an alabaster jar of very expensive perfume, made of pure nard. She broke the jar and poured the perfume on his head.

Some of those present were saying indignantly to one another "Why this waste of perfume? . . ."

"Leave her alone," said Jesus . . . . "She did what she could . . ."

MARK 14:3-8

Just wait till you see your great-grandmother's grave," my second cousins told me as we toured the Eastern Townships on a roots tour several years ago. "Your great-grandfather was considered quite an important man in his day, but your great-grandmother worked her fingers to the bone running a big boarding house while he traveled around being important, and when she died—well, you just won't believe what he put on her headstone."

"Yeah," snorted the other cousin, not able to wait until we got there for me to share in her indignation. "He put, 'She did the best she could.'" Such faint praise, I agreed, did seem less than such a woman had deserved. Suddenly I could not wait to see Great-grandmother Louisa's headstone.

Later that day, when we walked respectfully on the cemetery grass up to the headstone of my great-grandmother, I got my camera ready to capture the inscription I had been told about. Then I lowered it and read the words again. There, engraved in stone, was not the phrase, "She did the best she could," but Jesus' words of approbation at Mary's poured-out love: "She hath done what she could," one of the loveliest phrases in the Bible (Mark 14:8 KJV).

As I suggested recently to a graduating class of a Canadian seminary, perhaps one way that we can make good choices among the opportunities that present themselves is by asking ourselves what a summation of our lives might look like. "Always Busy" would scarcely be a distinguished epitaph, after all. And there is no room on a headstone for a resumé, however distinguished.

The Bible, of course, records the summing up phrases of many lives. Enoch "walked with God." Abraham was "the friend of God." Noah would have needed a whole cairn to record that he was "a righteous man, blameless among the people of his time, and he walked with God."

The exploits of David's mighty men are recounted in brief, chilling phrases counting enemy heads, and the reigns and characters of the kings are summarized with clear-headed judgment. King Rehoboam, who "did evil because he had not set his heart on seeking the Lord," is contrasted with Asa, whose "heart was fully committed to the Lord all his life." Or there is King Jehoram who, we are told, "passed away, to no one's regret."

In the New Testament, the summaries are spoken by the subjects themselves. There is Paul's "I have fought the good

44

fight, I have finished the race, I have kept the faith" and John's "I, John, your brother and companion in the suffering and the kingdom and the patient endurance that are ours in Jesus." And there is Jesus' summary of his ministry as he renders his accounting as a steward: "I have brought you glory...by completing the work you gave me to do."

With such examples, what would I want to be the keynote of my life, the phrase that would sum it all up? The word that occurs to me is "faithful"—faithful in seeking to know God far beyond intellectualizing about him, deep into an obedient and loving relationship, becoming the kind of worshipper the Father seeks, worshipping in spirit and truth.

I would want to be, throughout the span of my life, faithful in seeking to hear and to do the Word of God, to handle honestly and lovingly the book that directs and corrects the people of God from one generation to another. I would want to be faithful in fellowship with a local body of believers, the visible representation of the invisible church. And I would want to be found faithful in seeking to find ways to communicate the good news that "God was in Christ, reconciling the world to himself," adapting methods and language to the media and idiom of our day, but never compromising the content of the great story of God's intervention "for us and for our salvation."

When my work is brought to a conclusion, I want to be remembered as one whose "heart was set on pilgrimage," one who blessed the countryside through which I passed, discovering springs of joy in the Valleys of Weeping along the way (Psalm 84).

Models for me include two of my beloved friends whose earthly memento is a shared headstone in the quiet churchyard of a tiny Anglican church near our farm. I went there the other night to think about their lives and to remember. They were lovely in their Christ-filled, Christ-focused and Christ-directed lives and lovely in their love for each other. Now Robert and Joy McKerihan's earthly remains lie side-by-side in a churchyard sweet with the scent of lilacs and sheltered by a soldiery of ragged spruce.

The inscription on their shared stone reminds me that only their dust is there—not themselves—death for them not an end but a consummation. The words on the stone do not praise them, but point beyond them to the hope that drew them forward through life and through death. "With Christ, which is far better."

What do I hope one day will be remembered of me when I, too, am "with Christ" in that final way? "Faithful in her generation."

Or perhaps I should suggest that my family borrow the inscription from my great-grandmother's grave and have it declared, even if misunderstood, that "She hath done what she could."

9

GOLD FROM THE FIRE

But he knows the way I take;
When he has tested me,
I will come forth as gold.

JOB 23:10

To those who have grown up hearing the Bible read and taught, this image from Job is familiar, where testing and trouble serve as refining fires in which the precious metal of godly character is heated out of the surrounding ore and poured, pure and molten, into ingot moulds. Similarly, as the Book of Proverbs says, "The crucible for silver and the furnace for gold, but the Lord tests the heart" (17:3). Appropriately enough, with Egypt a supplier of gold and other metals on the ancient trade ways, the time spent by the Hebrews in Egypt was seen as time spent in a smelting furnace. The Exodus was interpreted as the intentional removal of the purified metal from the furnace (see, for instance, Deut 4:20). In the Bible's economy, affliction purifies the best qualities in us.

Peter draws on these images from the Old Testament in his first letter to the persecuted Christians of Asia Minor: "For a little while you may have had to suffer grief in all kinds of trials. These have come so that your faith—of greater worth than gold, which perishes even though refined by fire—may be proved genuine and may result in praise, glory and honour when Jesus Christ is revealed" (1 Pt 1:6, 7).

One summer, I discovered a fresh Canadian image to remind me what it could mean to "come forth as gold." The withering heat had no counterpart of relieving rain. According to meteorological reports that year, our area had received only half of the normal precipitation since seeding time; our farm had received a much lower percentage of rainfall—less than 30 percent of what we ordinarily expected. As our crops deteriorated, we—along with the crops—found ourselves in a furnace of affliction.

Of course we prayed for rain, but no rain came. It might not have felt so personal had we not been able to see rain to the north and west of us, the clouds building up time and time again in the late afternoon, giving us hope, the horizon blackening with lightning-streaked clouds, and the dark rain dropping like a curtain just "over there." We seemed to be under an inverted Red Sea, with the waters visibly parting to left and right, our crops struggling in dry ground.

The last two weeks of July I was teaching a summer school course in Vancouver, where one warm sunny day followed another, with no sign of any wet blanket of Pacific air to promise rain a couple of days later over our farm. Cam called me one morning to report that the night before he had driven back to the farm from a neighbouring community through a storm that grew more intense as he got closer to home. Finally, with rain falling so hard that the windshield washers could not keep the windshield clear, he dared to hope again for rain. The rain continued to within half a mile of our fence line, then abruptly stopped. Cam drove up to our home on a dusty, dry lane.

Throughout those long summer months there seemed a deliberate denial to us of necessary rain. When rain did finally fall in the first week of August, it seemed too late to make much difference for our crops. All the theological questions about the purpose and efficacy of prayer, about the ways in which God intervenes—or does not—in creation became our questions. Abstract theological statements could not answer the very real sense we had that an omnipotent God could have chosen to bless us with rain and did not.

Of course we knew that others were suffering—and had suffered—in similar ways, and not only brothers and sisters on farms. "Downsizing" was costing friends their long-held jobs; government cutbacks were making positions "redundant" and pushing people into premature retirement. We knew, too, that the "whole creation has been groaning as in the pains of childbirth right up to the present time," as Paul writes in Romans 8:22.

And that summer, we joined in its groaning. We saw the cereal crops head out, pitiful and ragged; we walked into the fields and found the field peas drying up from roots with only a few pods formed on each plant. Wearily and methodically, we prepared to go through the motions of harvest.

We started by harvesting the field-peas. Usually the combine collects just a little produce as you start down a swath, then a little more, and then, on a good year, there is a steady flow of grain. This time, there were a few peas pinging around, flung by the auger into the combine bin, and then a few more. There was no flow, no steady river of crop pouring into the hopper. When we moved out of the field, we knew that the crop we had harvested had not come close to covering the cost of its production.

The barley was somewhat better, yielding about half of a normal yield. And then, weary in heart and feeling emotionally as well as financially battered, we moved into the wheat field. The crop had looked so short and straggly that we had little hope. But as we began to combine the wheat, we saw a trickle of grain come up the auger and then turn into a steady flow of hard, bright kernels of wheat—far beyond what we could have imagined the short heads and thin stand would yield.

Tested in the flame of drought and heat, that wheat had "come forth as gold." We put kernels between our teeth and chewed them. We scooped up kernels and held them in our cupped hands, then spread our fingers and let the cool seed flow between them. It was, we sensed, the best quality wheat we had ever harvested. When samples were graded, our guess was verified; we had a premium grade of wheat, Number One, with extra-high protein.

And we realized that if we came through this year of reversal as well as the wheat had done, we would be doing fine.

10

Double Exposure

And we know that in all things God works for the good of those who love him, who have been called according to his purpose.

ROMANS 8:28

We once got a roll of film back that had been passed through the camera twice, and the series of double exposures created a rather interesting—if entirely unintended—effect. Faces on top of faces, winter on top of the previous summer, outdoor scenes glimpsed through windows in indoor scenes. And although we'll win no prizes with the pictures, they are fascinating to study, for the passage of time is caught in the montage.

Children and puppies have grown; a family member no longer with us smiles at the edges of pictures, her image swimming up through transparent children in snowsuits. The wedding that was about to happen has happened; last year's birthdays underlie this year's. Such "pleats in time" (as the American writer Walker Percy calls them) allow us to take note of changes and repetitions, the things that are unalterably different and the things that are reliably the same.

I experienced such a "pleat in time," or double exposure, once when I turned to my Bible during a particularly difficult time, when stress had reached a new kind of intensity.

As I prayed, a verse of Scripture began to sing its refrain in my head: "Make us glad according to the days wherein thou hast afflicted us." I turned to the passage in a Bible that lay at hand, one given to me long ago as a thank you gift from a group of young people with whom I had worked. There, in Psalm 90, was the whole text:

> Make us glad according to the days wherein thou hast afflicted us, and the years wherein we have seen evil. Let thy work appear unto thy servants, and thy glory unto their children. And let the beauty of the Lord our God be upon us: and establish thou the work of our hands upon us; yea, the work of our hands establish thou it. (Ps 90:15–17, KJV).

There was a note and a date in my handwriting in the margin adjacent to the verses: "My Prayer Today."

And suddenly, I was looking at that ancient prayer in the Psalms through a double exposure: the present situation underlaid by memories of that fall, fifteen years earlier when we had just come through several major family illnesses even as falling cattle prices wiped out our cattle feeding business and an August frost destroyed our crops. Then, too, crushed and bewildered, I had prayed the ancient prayer: "Make us glad according to the days wherein thou hast afflicted us."

And God had done so much more than make it fair. The next fifteen years of our lives had been fruitful ones. I realized as I looked at the date in the margin of my Bible how God had "let [his] work appear unto [his] servants." We had rebuilt our family farm business, seen our children grow into adulthood, been eyewitnesses to the renewal of a village church. We had taught the Scriptures and seen lives and families transformed.

What God had taught us provided the background experience for books and articles, including some that grew directly out of our personal pain. We had been blessed in every way.

Then came heavy weather again: a new financial crisis in agriculture threatened our livelihood; grief struck in new and unexpected ways; and many of our friends in the church were suffering through personal crises.

But as I looked at the prayer in the Psalms through the double exposure of the present pressure and the difficult times past, I saw that the faithfulness of God was what I really remembered.

There had been strength for each day—one day at a time—and the resources out of which to minister—to one person at a time. Despite the financial pressures of those days, our children grew up well nourished and well cherished to go out into life aware of the faithful provision of a loving God.

With each new crisis, these "pleats in time" help to remind me that I will survive the season of tears, God's way of preparing a seed-bed for new life. I will again be made glad.

11

Under the Rod

"I will bring you into the desert…and there, face to face, I will execute judgment upon you…I will take note of you as you pass under my rod, and I will bring you into the bond of the covenant"

Ezekiel 20:32–37

So many things had gone wrong one year, that when our teenage son came in to report yet another machinery breakdown he stood at the landing and called for his dad: "Is Job home?"

Later, Cam said, perplexed, "I don't know why God is doing this to us." I was theologically precise in my response: "He is not *doing* it to us; he is *allowing* it into our lives."

Cam pressed past my religious rhetoric, as he often does: "Listen: if God could prevent this from happening and doesn't, then it's all the same to me as if he were doing it."

Like Job, Cam pushed past the naturalistic explanations of Sabeans and Chaldeans, winds, firestorms and sickness to take his case straight to top: "The Lord gave and the Lord has taken away" (Job 1:21). Like Naomi, he brushed aside comforting platitudes to state the truth baldly: "The Lord has afflicted me; the Almighty has brought misfortune upon me" (Ruth 1:21).

When we experience pain, we tend to look everywhere for explanations—and to everyone for comfort—rather than tracing our problem back to the hand of God. For every believer, however, there is the experience of the rod of instruction and correction that leads to full maturity in the faith. Such discipline is no fun, but it is neither to be taken lightly nor resisted, since it is by such discipline that God defines and develops those who are his and brings them into fellowship with himself.

In a striking passage the prophet Ezekiel addresses God's people: "You say, 'We want to be like the nations, like the peoples of the world.'" And then Ezekiel speaks God's words of saving judgment in response: "But what you have in mind will never happen...I will bring you into the desert...and there, face to face, I will execute judgment upon you...*I will take note of you as you pass under my rod, and I will bring you into the bond of the covenant*" (Ezek 20:32–37).

God promises to preserve the identity of his people and to bring them into covenantal love with himself by means of judgment and correction, which is also salvation. There is—and always has been—a danger that our identity as a people of God should be lost, that our distinctness of attitude and the accent that betrays us as companions of the Nazarene should become blurred and indistinguishable from the world. It is God's discipline that spares us from such a terrible integration. For God is still calling out a people to himself with whom he can deal trustingly and truthfully within the "bond of the covenant."

"I will take note of you as you pass under my rod." Of what may God take note as we pass under his rod? For one thing, of our attitude toward his discipline. A weary, resentful, bitter attitude will render us less useful as a result of chastisement, rather than more useful, and the enemy of our souls will take every opportunity to foster our natural rebellion during times of correction.

God also takes note of our attitude towards him: an angry rejection of the disciplining rod denies God's sovereign right to shape and train those he has chosen as his own. Such an attitude will ultimately rob us of the joy of fellowship into which we are invited as we pass under the rod.

What God ultimately takes note of is that we are, indeed, his own. And as we pass under that rod, the amazing truth of being called to be his people and the sheep of his pasture dawns deeply within our spirits. This present buffeting, this discipline, this apparently denied request—these are not the signs that he has cast us off, but that he has chosen us and intends that we should bear the full weight of his glory; the proof that he is, indeed, able to "sanctify to us our deepest distress."

It is only under the rod that we pass into "the bond of the covenant," the love-bond with which God binds himself to us but which, in our fallenness and proneness to sin, we so often fail to understand. Chastened, delivered, judged, we are brought out from the social pressures that endanger us with conformity. Our identity as children of God is fully assured. And we find ourselves in a new, more deeply blessed relationship with God: the relationship of a bond of love and trust in which we not only can safely trust God, but in which he can increasingly trust us.

Is it worth it? The writer of the Book of Hebrews affirms that it is, drawing together a number of Old Testament passages on God's chastening rod, and concluding: "No discipline seems pleasant for the time, but painful. Later on, however, it produces a harvest of righteousness and peace for those who have been trained by it" (Heb 12:11).

When we go through the hard times, the times when we feel God's rod of correction, training, reproof and punishment, we live towards that "later on." Then one day we discover that we have entered more fully than ever before into the covenant of love into which Jesus came to call us. And we can say, and really mean: "Your rod and your staff, they comfort me" (Ps 23:4).

12

SHORT, COLD DAYS

*I have learned the secret of being content in any and every
situation, whether well fed or hungry, whether living in
plenty or in want. I can do everything through him who gives
me strength.*

PHILIPPIANS 4:12

Somewhere along the way, I must admit to having mislaid
my enthusiasm for winter. I can remember when my hands
would tingle as we tobogganed down wind-sculpted drifts
or carved out snow caves under them. I can remember one
wonderful, terrible prairie winter in Briercrest, Saskatchewan
when the snowdrifts were so high we bundled-up children could
pose for pictures sitting on top of telephone poles.

From that winter I have all the classic Canadian winter
memories: riding in a horse-drawn sleigh, cosy under a buffalo
robe; shouting to hear the eerie echoes in blue ice-tunnels
prepared to drain the melt-water away from farm buildings.

From my Alberta childhood winters I have memories that
always involve skates: second-hand skates, usually with black
boots. And from my Lethbridge winters, most memorably, the
magical shape of hope: a Chinook arch pale and clear over Chief

Mountain, and the sudden Pacific warmth flowing down over our winter days. Those days we lost the mittens we had worn to school in the morning because by the time we came home, who needed them?

But time has passed, and my hands ache now when the weather turns cold, and I really do not like January very much. Maybe because, like the Roman God for whom it is named, it is two-faced, looking both wearily back to the year that is past and warily forward to the year that lies ahead.

My personal new year coincides better with the Jewish *Rosh Hashanah* in the fall: when school starts, when harvest nears completion, when we can look ahead to the work of the fall and winter months. The outburst of light and joy that comes with Christmas carries us through the ever-lengthening darkness of December.

Then, when the last candle of the advent wreath is blown out, we are in the cold darkness of January. In central Alberta the sun comes up briefly with little warmth; the light that comes through frosted windows is wan and yellow. Night falls before the school buses finish their runs.

The darkness and the cold cannot be ignored. One dreams, of course, of escape. I am embarrassed, now, to remember arguing some years ago with a friend that she should not move from a northern state to California, quoting Samuel Rutherford who said, "Grace groweth best in the winter." For those with the means and the freedom from schedules, a winter-free retreat becomes a very attractive way of dealing with this time of year.

But escape is not always possible, and return is usually necessary. For many, if not for most of us, there have to be other ways to cope. This year I am wondering if I can remember—or perhaps relearn, through my little granddaughters—how to embrace the season instead of resisting it. Evenings this year, we will draw the heavy drapes early to shut out the darkness and cold and celebrate the early dark with a fire in the woodstove and books read aloud and cups of warm cocoa before their bedtime. What we cannot avoid we can embrace.

And I shall try not only to embrace but also to enhance this season. I am discovering with each passing year how important color and design are to me. Especially in winter. Now I know that I love and hunger for color, and that through long, white winters, my feelings of well-being have been silently nourished by the huge green plants my husband tends in our living-dining room. And now I, too, find myself tending plants. I choose ones that flower. I love watching buds swell and flowers explode into color and pattern.

And what I am going to do with January this year is what I want to learn to do with life in general: the many difficult spaces from which there is no escape (and we all sometimes echo the cry, "Oh that I had the wings of a dove; I would fly away and be at peace"—Psalm 55:6) I want to embrace and to enhance. For to everything there is a season.

Somewhere between the twentieth of January and the twentieth of February, I begin to notice a tiny seepage of light back into the emptied cup of the sky, and of joy into my spirit. And with George Herbert, I am amazed:

> How fresh, O Lord, how sweet and clean
> Are thy returns! ...
> Who would have thought my shrivel'd heart
> Could have recover'd greennesse?

13

SAD JOY, GLAD SORROW

He will wipe every tear from their eyes. There will be no more death or mourning or crying or pain, for the old order of things has passed away.

REVELATION 21:4

It took me all four of our children's weddings, but I think I am finally beginning to understand what weddings are all about.

The ceremony, of course, I understood, and the need for witnesses who represent not only the two families but the whole people of God. But what about the elaboration of that into a major event? I think I get it now.

At its best, a wedding celebration is the earthly echo of heaven's joy at the formation of a new union of love, a potentially procreative unit of human society.

But every joy here on earth is an alloy. And the other main purpose of the wedding celebration is to overwhelm grief with a great joy. For there is sorrow in a wedding, too. There is a crisis of aging for parents, together with the sorrow of the loss of a child.

The old cliché, "We're not losing a daughter; we're gaining a son," is—like most clichés—only half true. Parents both lose the primary allegiance of a son or daughter *and* gain a new family member with whom to forge a relationship. And young people both lose a home *and* create the nucleus of a new family unit.

When we began to understand that we were both joyfully anticipating the marriage and at the same time grieving, we understood the whole day better.

But more than that, I began to understand the purpose of the whole "joyful bother" of the celebration and found it to be profoundly Christian.

As the light that came into the world overwhelmed the darkness, as Jesus by his resurrection overwhelmed death, so in a wedding celebration joy overwhelms sorrow and begins the healing process as one family unit is cut apart to make a new one.

We had scarcely caught our breath from the energy outlay of one of our weddings when one of our closest friends died after open-heart surgery. At age fifty-three. As I turned from the telephone with the news of his death, I had a burst of tears and whispered, "Home free! Andy's home free." Then joy began to overwhelm sorrow. At the service of rejoicing for his life and home-calling, we realized again how deeply joy and sorrow, on this side, are intermixed.

Sorrow overwhelmed by joy. It's a redemption principle. Jesus speaks of it to his disciples in his "comforting discourse" in John 16:21–22: "A woman giving birth to a child has pain because her time has come; but when her baby is born she forgets the anguish because of her joy that a child is born into the world.

So with you: Now is your time of grief, but I will see you again and you will rejoice, and no one will take away your joy."

Using similar imagery, the writer to the Hebrews says that Jesus "for the joy set before him endured the cross" (Heb 12:2). The joy set before him—the overwhelming joy of one day saying to the Father, "Here am I, and the children God has given me" (Heb 2:13)—sustained Jesus in his soul-struggle on the way to the cross.

I can imagine Jesus, as he pondered his impending death, meditating on Isaiah 53:11, staying his heart on the closing prophecy, "He will see the travail of his soul, and shall be satisfied." The thought of the church he would bring forth sustained Jesus on the way to the cross just as the thought of the child brought to birth sustains the travail of a mother.

What Jesus accomplished at the cross was not the annihilation of evil but the overwhelming of evil with good, not the end of hate but the triumph over it by love. The resurrection both demonstrated and provided the means by which the greatest sorrow that the curse of sin has inflicted—the loss of loved ones to death—can be overwhelmed by the joy of knowing that for those who "die in the Lord," death opens on a new, eternal mode of being.

It is no accident that in John's great Revelation, the consummation of Christ's redemptive work is realized as a marriage celebration: "Blessed are those who are invited to the wedding supper of the Lamb!" (Rev 19:9). The overwhelming of the sorrow, both of the Lord of the church and of the suffering church through the ages, by the great joy of union with the Saviour is the essence of that great celebration.

The funeral of each of our brothers and sisters in Christ is the celebration of their having received their wedding invitations. And the marriage celebration of every believing couple is a foreshadowing on earth of that great celebration in heaven. Funerals and weddings both are reminders that here joy and sorrow are deeply intertwined. But each, in its own way, reminds us that one day grief will be swallowed up by Christ's victory. And we will know pure, unalloyed joy.

Wailing Walls, Waiting Walls

Reflections on the Church & Scripture

14

WAILING WALLS, WAITING WALLS

*"You will call your walls Salvation
and your gates Praise."*

ISAIAH 60:18

When we turned the sod for our new church, we had a village celebration suffused by joy. The service was held outdoors at the site of our new church building. Of course, no glass cathedral was envisioned—just a simple building big enough to shelter a sturdy rural congregation from the severe Alberta weather.

Sun-warmed and heart-warmed, we sat in the twinkling shade of the white poplars at the corner of the new property, listening to those who spoke and sang of a love that touched and changed their lives, a love known through this church family. We sensed the Spirit's presence in and around us, heard God speak to us through the Word preached by a newly called young pastor. Then, over a plenteous potluck picnic, we visited and reminisced and rejoiced.

But lingering in my mind throughout the day were the words of a friend who had called a few days earlier. I mentioned the church-building project to him.

"I'm glad for you," he said. "But I'm not at all sure you're not doing something crazy, building a church. Sometimes I think we should quit building churches and start building wailing walls."

I laughed, of course, but just a shade uneasily. His quip raised all the spectres that haunt any congregation contemplating a building project: visions of "half-finished towers"—those terrible, half-finished church buildings—or, just a terrible, only half-paid-for mega-projects from which the initiating vision has departed; visions of a congregation divided over something as trivial as the colour of the carpet; and always, visions of the hungry people who could be fed or the Bibles that could be printed, even with our small budget.

Should we be building a church building at all? This one—or any one? Or is our friend right? Would wailing walls be more worthy undertakings?

For sure, there are lots of things to wail about: the failure of the church as whole to meet the needs of our communities, our personal failure to fully understand and apply the gospel in all of its shocking simplicity in our own lives and relationships, the whole groaning, travailing, polluted and exploited creation, the silenced cries of the unborn who die before they get a chance to live, the stifled weeping of abused, neglected, or rejected women or men, the unrealized potential for God's glory in all of us.

And for sure, we could do with some good, sound weepers within our Christian community. Some like Mrs. Greenleaf, the Flannery O'Connor character who each day "cut all the morbid stories out of the newspaper ... took these to the woods and dug a hole and buried them and then ... fell on the ground over them and mumbled and groaned for an hour or so." Overheard, her prayer was found to consist of one repeated word, "Jesus! Jesus!" (*Complete Stories*, p. 316).

Mrs. Greenleaf, excessive and grotesque as she is, is nonetheless portrayed by O'Connor as a source of life, caring and renewal, in a cold dead world of self-interest. We need more Christians like her: people who can share with God in his grief over a self-destructive world.

We could well rediscover the weeping of true repentance, too. I believe that the biggest single obstacle to effective evangelism is not the indifference or hostility of the unbelievers, but the lack of real repentance experienced by believers. Those who consider themselves Christians, but who have never sorrowed over the sinful condition of their own hearts, have little care or compassion for others.

Repentance unlocks us, unbends us, lets us enter into our identity as fallen, faulty humans. At the same time, real repentance grants us a new kind of joy in the fullness of God's forgiveness that impels us to share—not from an elevated, "we-have-the-truth-for-you-poor-folk" position, but from a shoulder-to-shoulder stance: "Here is saving truth for all of us poor folk."

So yes: we could do with some wailing walls. Perhaps we should so designate one wall of every new church building. But it is not an either/or proposition. We need to go on building churches to house the life of our congregations, churches that open invitationally into our communities and that are built in response to our communities' needs, glass cathedrals in the symbolic sense of being open, transparent and wholly vulnerable and accountable.

And we need to remember that we are building not only wailing walls, but also waiting walls. One day, between one hammer blow and the next, the moment of transformation will occur. The church, now partial, visible, imperfect, around which we need to erect walls, will become the church completed, universal, perfected—no longer needing human-built walls.

All the walls we build now are but waiting walls—waiting for the day of final redemption when God's kingdom is fully realized in Christ's return, when

> No longer will violence be heard in your land,
> nor ruin or destruction within your borders,
> but you will call your walls Salvation
> and your gates Praise.

Someday, some church will get only half-built, not because of uncounted cost, but because of the shout announcing our returning Lord. Maybe it will be yours.

Even so, come, Lord Jesus.

15

OUT OF TIME

Be very careful, then, how you live—not as unwise, but as
wise, making the most of every opportunity. . . .
EPHESIANS 5:15-16

I don't apologize for being busy. But once in a while I like to check to be sure that I am spending time on the things that really matter.

I have just gone through my familiar time-management exercise one more time, recording daily what I do with my time for a couple of weeks. I use different coloured markers to see what time I spend meeting personal and family needs, serving the local church and community and working in my office. When I look at the total hours spent on each type of activity over a couple of weeks, I realize that despite my more or less continuous sense of frustration with the limitations of time, the time I spend does pretty accurately reflect my priorities.

I believe in sober stewardship of the limited resources of our lives—time, energy, money—on the basis that "we are not our own" (1 Cor 6:19). We have been purchased lock, stock and barrel for the King's higher purposes. So each day I make up a plan from my "on my mind to do" list. I work against deadlines and set goals. But I also offer it all up to the Lord—day, plan, energy and the as-yet-unknown interruptions that may be the day's real appointments. I seek to know and respond to those nudges that push me out of my planned trajectory more fully into the Spirit's.

Over the years, I have learned a few principles about time that go beyond "time management"—with its illusion of control—and take the time of my life in the direction of eternity.

Time Stretching—One winter noon in Toronto, a friend helped me find a winter coat and take it to a seamstress to be shortened, all in time to take it with me on my five o'clock flight home after the afternoon's television taping. We did all this in the three-quarters of an hour left over after a business lunch.

Our shopping trip did not start well. I could not find the shop that had been suggested to me. "There's no way we have the time to get this done," I said.

"You have all the time you need," she said. "Time is flexible, not solid." In a couple of minutes, she told me that she had learned from Canadian aboriginals the concept of "time stretching."

"Just take a deep breath," she told me, "and say to yourself, 'I have all the time I need.' Envision time as elastic and make it stretch around what you need to get done." It worked that day and has worked innumerable times for me since. I'm not sure how mysterious the process is. It may be simply that the lovely concept of long curves of time calms me and lets me function effectively. But time stretching is one of the ways I cope when pressure threatens effectiveness.

Time Multiplication—I discovered "time multiplication" when a woman next to me at a conference commented, "You know there is such a lot said about how money given to God

72

is multiplied back to the giver. But few ever mention how time given to God is multiplied in much the same way."

The concept is the five loaves and two small fishes story, over and over again. Time offered to Christ in loving worship and service, seems to be given back to us in a clear and quiet sense of order, in increased efficiency and in multiplied effectiveness.

Time Redemption—In Ephesians 5:15, Paul refers to time redemption. He says, "Redeem the time, because the days are evil" (KJV). When we redeem time, we convert it from the mercantile commodity exchange system of the world into eternal coinage so that time becomes the means by which we open up eternity for others. The time it takes to make a phone call, build a friendship, care for a little Sunday school class or visit a person can become an investment that has an eternal effect in the life of another human being.

Time Lifting—One of the times when I most clearly notice how flexible time really is happens on the rare Sunday morning when I miss going to church. Have you ever noticed how insignificant an hour spent at home on a Sunday morning actually is, compared to how expansive and significant that same hour is when it is spent with the people of God in the presence of God?

On the Lord's Day, when we celebrate it by "assembling ourselves together," we move into a totally different economy, one in which time and money are not exchangeable as commodities but where both are offered in worship and so touch on the edge of eternity. In Sabbath quiet, the grandeur of God's plan and purpose is for a few moments almost graspable, and the curtain of time that separates us from eternity lifts for just a little while.

One day the great angel will declare that we are out of time (Rev 10:6). Until then, the time we spend in personal devotion and corporate worship gives us a foretaste of what lies ahead. For a few moments the curtain of time rises and we glimpse eternity.

The English poet Henry Vaughan (1621–95) wrote,

> I saw Eternity the other night
> Like a great Ring of pure and endless light,
> All calm as it was bright,
> And round beneath it, Time in hours, days, years
> Driv'n by the spheres
> Like a vast shadow moved.

As we live in this "vast shadow" called time, we need to remember that our ultimate place of being is that "great Ring of pure and endless light" which is eternity. The "hours, days, years" that often seem fragmented and disjointed can be thoughtfully managed with this reality in mind.

16

DENOMINATIONAL VAGABOND

I appeal to you, brothers, in the name of our Lord Jesus Christ, that all of you agree with one another so that there may be no divisions among you and that you may be perfectly united in mind and thought.

1 CORINTHIANS 1:10

We call ourselves "Christian," but one of our favourite ways of categorizing people is by denomination. We have developed the casual question, "What church do you belong to?" into a sociometric tool, a way of quickly placing a person on a scale. We can tell spiritual temperature (Pentecostal= hot; Presbyterian=cool), doctrinal clarity (Baptist=crystalline; Community Church=murky) even ethnic background (Lutheran=German or Scandinavian; Anglican=Anglo or African). If we've been in the splintered circles of evangelicalism very long, we can pretty well construct a personality profile of a person on the basis of the answer to one simple question.

This really makes it confusing for people when they try to get a handle on my personal or doctrinal preferences by means of asking that question. I am a denominational vagabond—which is *not*, I want to emphasize, the same as a "church tramp."

Let me explain. My very earliest memories of worship are in a Plymouth Brethren assembly; I remember the folding chairs and the white cloth, clearly marked with fold lines, on the plain table where the bread and the cup were set out. For the rest of my growing-up years my faith found its formation in the Christian and Missionary Alliance, with its emphasis on the Spirit's work in both the personal and global realms.

After our marriage, Cam and I continued to be active in that denomination for nearly fifteen years, until we responded to neighbours' requests to come and help in a tiny United Church in a village near our farm. And so we found ourselves "mainline Protestants," a somewhat startling experience after having viewed the world from the front doors of "tabernacles" for the first half of our lives.

As evangelicals within the United Church in some of its most turbulent history, we came into contact with a splendid band of committed believers and also got back in touch with deep Methodist family roots in both of our families: Cam's family having come from the Bible Christian Movement, a Methodist renewal movement in Devon, and my great-grand-father having been a Methodist preacher and church planter in the Eastern Townships of Quebec.

When our small community church made its decision to break ties with the United Church after the 1988 General Council, our links with all denominations were broken, even though we were still attending the same local church. We were post-denominational.

During winters when we have lived away from our home community, we have enjoyed the fellowship of a variety of churches: warm-hearted Baptist churches, a university-embracing Evangelical Free Church and now a quiet, conservative Anglican church. At the same time, the small community church where our farm is located was also exploring its "spiritual kinship" with a range of denominations, finally deciding on a affiliation with the Evangelical Free Church.

So when you ask me, "What church do you go to?" you may not be able to categorize me quite as neatly as is convenient. I love and rejoice in the work of the Spirit of God wherever that self-directed wind chooses to blow. I speak to gatherings of many denominations and in many inter-denominational settings. I seek to be faithful to the Word within "the whole family" (as Paul calls the church in Ephesians 3:15) and accountable within a local congregation.

Does that make me pre-, post- or mid-denominational?

I hope it makes me trans-denominational. In our culture, increasingly indifferent as it is to religious distinctions and increasingly hostile to dogma, we will make an impact only as we identify with one another in our common calling under Christ, valuing and claiming our shared discipleship more than our denominational distinctives.

I remember from my early childhood being part of a little gathering of believers that met in a church hall behind the Stern Furniture store in Lethbridge, Alberta. There, in Sunday evening services, we sang a chorus to the tune of "Red River Valley":

> I don't care what church you belong to,
> Just as long as for Calvary you stand;
> And if your heart's been washed in the fountain,
> You're my brother, come give me your hand.

The singing went along with a good brisk round of handshaking and introductions—with "brother" being changed to "sister" as appropriate—the whole process not too dissimilar to what in my Anglican church is called "Passing the Peace."

I am grateful for denominations, for the administrative and interlinking work that is done on behalf of local congregations. Just a few years as an "independent community church" showed our local village congregation how necessary it is to be "plugged in" to some larger whole, not just mystically, knowing that we are part of one "holy catholic church," but actually—having sister churches and missions to connect with, being challenged by the needs of others beyond our own community, finding pastors whose training and vision of the church are similar to that of our community and congregation.

I am grateful for the way denominations maintain doctrinal distinctives and entertain important theological discussions. But you cannot do a personality profile on me by asking, "What church do you belong to?"

On the other hand, maybe you can.

18

SOMETIMES A
LIGHT SURPRISES

Let the word of Christ dwell in you richly as you teach and admonish one another with all wisdom, and as you sing psalms, hymns and spiritual songs with gratitude in your hearts to God.

COLOSSIANS 3:16

We stand to sing, "A Mighty Fortress is Our God." And I wonder how many congregations, in how many different kinds of buildings, accompanied by pipe organs or electronic ones, pianos, guitars or bands or orchestras, will sing this same hymn this Sunday. Or next.

This morning I am in Knox Evangelical Free Church in Edmonton, a congregation that conducts its non-liturgical worship in a square, high vaulted sanctuary constructed for Presbyterians. As we sing, our voices sheltered by the strength of the pipe organ, I think of how the Scandinavian roots of the Free Church intertwine with the Scottish roots of the Presbyterian-style structure as we sing Luther's great hymn expressing the spirit of the German Reformation. I am struck by the way that hymn music represents the unity of the body of Christ over time, even while maintaining the distinctiveness of the cultural context in which it is written, every hymn a sort of time-capsule, a gift from a worshipping community in a particular moment in space and time to the larger and longer community of the church as a whole over time and space.

Unity. Continuity. Poetry and music born in cultural contexts and then becoming songs that transcend both their makers and the circumstances of their making. I have a chance to think more about it all when, the next Sunday, I worship at Yorkminster Park Baptist Church in Toronto. If there is such a thing as "high Baptist," this is it, with the choral processional, introit and responses, and a superb soloist. We sing of God's "ceaseless, unexhausted love" as written by Charles Wesley and share the depression-tormented William Cowper's wonder that "Sometimes a light surprises/The Christian while he sings"— these eighteenth-century hymns still warm with revival. Again the traditions and history of the church become ours in the music in which we participate as a congregation.

After the service I discover that I have been singing these historic hymns just across the aisle from Margaret Clarkson, our own Canadian hymn writer, whose hymns, already included in many hymnals, will be sung in other congregations a hundred years from now—two hundred, three hundred—until Jesus comes. Continuity being extended, enriched, added to by the ongoing creativity of today's composers and writers. Congregations trying out music, sifting it by using it, adding to repertoire and quickly dropping what becomes stale with repetition, lack of melody or shallow words in an ongoing process of canon formation to which our hymnbooks, chorus supplements and overhead projectors bear witness.

"Singing and making melody in our hearts to the Lord." The hymns carry not only the history of the church but also our own personal histories in the faith. Recently I was in a service during which the congregation broke into a spontaneous *a cappella* rendition after the rector said, "Remember that song we used to sing in Sunday school, 'Jesus bids us shine...'" Research on the return of "baby boomers" to the church suggests that remembered music is one of the appeals.

Hymns signal our personal and communal history, our creativity as a people of God, our distinctiveness and our unity, and they express our fundamental harmony. Behind me, all around me are people who really do know how to sing. Some are singing parts, filling in the bass, the tenor and alto. I am among the sturdy yeoman singers who carry the melody. We need each other, those parts-singers and we who sing in unison. The whole song is not an alto line, nor a descant. Nor can the whole song be sung by the bass or tenor. The whole song requires the resources of the whole congregation, and it makes me think about the richness of the church when all of God's people are given full voice.

Where else in any Canadian city except in the churches do groups of people, anywhere from a hundred to a thousand voices strong, get a chance to sing together without rehearsing? In an increasingly specialized world in which only the most talented in any field get any opportunity to use their gifts, on every Sunday, *I* get a chance to sing! I can sing heartily, and I do.

Some three million evangelical Christians worship in Canada each Sunday morning. Parcelled out in small congregations and large, we are making music. It's not great music, often, but in the deepest sense of the word it is *good* music: music that needs to be sung by people who need to be singing.

The very best in church music is not the music presented by the choir or the visiting musical team. The best in church music is the music we make together as, Sunday by Sunday, we celebrate our heritage, our history and our glorious future as the people of God.

18

THE RHETORIC-REALITY GAP

We know that the whole creation has been groaning as in the pains of childbirth up to the present time. Not only so, but we ourselves . . . groan inwardly as we wait eagerly for . . . the redemption of our bodies. For in this hope we are saved.

ROMANS 8:22-24

One of the things I noticed during the first phase of the spiritual renewal of our little village church was the honesty, unblunted by an acquired Christian language, with which people spoke their minds.

I remember especially the night we were working on "Amazing Grace" at choir practice. One of the sopranos objected to the phrase, "that saved a wretch like me," suggesting that we substitute, "that calls us to be free." At the time, I was appalled at her suggestion, though I tried not to show it.

But the other day the incident came to mind, and I wondered if perhaps that woman was more honest than most of us are. She, quite frankly, had not yet experienced any conviction of sin that would make her feel "a wretch," and she recognized that the words described something quite different from her experience.

There are probably lines in a lot of hymns that we should be humming, at least some of the time; they say something we don't really mean or haven't really experienced. But we sing soulfully on because, all too soon after we have an experience of the reality of God, of salvation, of the presence of Christ in our lives, we get inducted into a rhetoric that can conceal from even ourselves the truth of what we think, what we believe, what we experience.

Once learned, this rather easy Christian rhetoric is not easy to unlearn. The other day I tried to phrase a "thanks, but no" response to a speaking invitation. I tore up three letters that said things such as, "In waiting on the Lord, I do not feel led to accept," before I managed to write a clear one-paragraph note that said, "I am not able to accept your invitation . . . ."

Why was it all so hard? Why does getting back to letting my "yes be yes and my no, no" make me sweat? I think it's because the evangelical Christian patter softens, sentimentalizes or spiritualises a lot of hard edges in our knobby, very human lives. It represents not what *is,* but what we think *should be.*

Perhaps I should anguish in prayer over every speaking invitation I receive. But generally speaking, I don't. I get a sort of feeling about whether or not a particular invitation is one I should accept. It is a feeling compounded of my personal and family situation at the time, the cutting edge I am interested in developing, and not uninfluenced by the location of the conference.

Does that amount to being Spirit-led? I hope so, of course. But I can close the rhetoric-reality gap by saying simply, "No thanks."

The rhetoric-reality gap occurs in our relationships as well. Christians tend to be a very zipped-up group of people. In the graduate student lounge at the university, you say to a colleague,

"How's it going?" and you are likely to hear, "Terrible!" or "I'm stuck with my writing. Let's go for coffee." It doesn't seem to cause anyone a problem to indicate that everything is not just perfect.

But at a church ask, "How's it going?" and you're almost sure to get a bright, tight, "Fine, thanks."

Of course, we say that to each other because we have learned that it is the only acceptable answer—the only one people want to hear. Want to hear, I suspect, because it confirms the "Everything's fine for *us Christians*" line we have managed to perpetuate in the face of all the evidence to the contrary.

This learned church language (let's not call it "Christian" any more) is a sort of adaptation we have developed to bridge the rough reality of life as we experience it and the idealized, blurry-eyed, sentimentalized form of Christianity that is all too often sung and preached.

"Come to Jesus, and everything will be all right," we say. People come to Jesus; they encounter him as Ultimate Reality. But everything does not become all right. Children get hurt, messed up with drugs, pregnant in their teens. A beloved family member dies of cancer. Or of AIDS.

"Kneel at the altar and receive this or that special blessing, and there will be no more struggle," we say or imply. And people kneel, then go away to do hour-to-hour combat with sins that are easier to give in to than to name. Instead of confronting the real pain and paradoxes of life, we offer a patter that covers the yawning gap between what we think the Christian experience ought to be and what it really is.

A woman struggling with health and marriage problems decided one Sunday she wouldn't lie. When a friendly greeter said, "And how are you today?" she replied, "Hurting, thank you." There wasn't even a pause as the hand-shaker murmured,

"That's wonderful. Praise the Lord!" and hurried to grasp another hand.

Hurting, thank you. And very, very human. That's what we Christians really are.

But have you ever noticed how much easier it is to tell a story of a solved problem than to go to a friend and ask for prayer? How much easier it is to form an opinion and back it up with a Scripture text or two than it is to admit honestly, "I don't know"? How much easier it is to invoke "the Lord's will" than to take responsibility for our decisions? How much easier it is just to sing those happy hymns than to hum or keep silent where they do not speak what we know or believe?

I'm trying to call myself up short on church rhetoric. I find the best way to close the rhetoric-reality gap is by means of plain, simple speech. Just like Jesus told us to speak in the first place.

When I spiritualise everything, I run the grave risk of taking the Lord's name in vain. And when I make things sound easy, I'm in danger of taking the promise that we are "more than conquerors" out of the context in which Paul himself placed it: the context of a groaning, pain-filled creation of which we are ourselves an aching part.

19

THE DEWBERRY BLESSING

Do not be afraid, little flock, for your Father has been pleased to give you the kingdom.

LUKE 12:32

As the days shorten and the cold deepens, we stack the cast-iron wood-burning stove in our living room full of deadfall wood and settle in for its long, slow burn. We don't burn anything special—punk poplar, sometimes spruce. Pulling a chair up close to the fire to rest my feet on the stone hearth, I think of how like this wood-burning stove is to our little village church.

Years ago a renewal began with the breath of the Spirit on a tiny village church with only a few sparks left in its grey ashes. The renewal started—if the work of the unseen Holy Spirit can be traced—with a women's Bible study. Women from the nearby community had phoned me and asked, "If we came to you, would you teach us the Word?" Weekly, a group of women gathered: mothers and mothers-in-law, daughters and daughters-in-law, grandmothers and granddaughters all in the same fellowship.

Some heard the good news about Jesus and became believers; others came into a fuller understanding of commitments they had made years earlier. These women began to yearn for their husbands and children to know the personal presence of the risen Christ. So Cam began to teach an adult Bible study class at the village church on Sundays, and because he was a farmer and not a preacher, men felt comfortable coming. One by one, family by family, "the Lord added to [our] number...those who were being saved" (Acts 2:47).

Now, all these yeas later, we can see that what began then was the beginning of a long, slow burn. The church has been in continuous renewal since that time. That does not mean it has been in a frenzy of spiritual excitement. There have been times in all of the believers' lives of deep stirring, times of steady plodding, and times of just barely hanging on.

The Dewberry Community Church will never rank with the "mega-churches" we read about, but there is a continual intake of new believers. On most Sundays there are concentric circles of people: "comers," "becomers" and "believers," with an inward spiraling motion towards the centre of faith in Jesus Christ and commitment to the body of believers.

Over such a long haul there are certain discernible patterns: a period of intake through many conversions is followed by a period of plateauing. This is a time for discipling and nurturing, a time when some who make beginnings with Christ fall away, become discouraged and indifferent, while others—in the midst of deep testing—ask the unanswerable, "Lord, to whom shall we go?" and carry on.

Then there follows a period of new ingathering, with new believers taking up the name of Jesus Christ as Lord. We have tried not to force enthusiasm just as we do not keep trying to re-light the stove while it still has a quiet glow, but rather we constantly feed the flame of love for Jesus just as we feed our fire.

We also early experienced a period of suspicion from the larger community, along with times since when it has seemed as though every family in the church was under severe pressure of one kind or another: emotional, or economic, or health issues besetting us. These are like the occasional times when the extreme cold of a winter day has formed a heat inversion over our chimney, keeping the smoke from rising up the chimney and forcing it down into our living room. Choking and coughing, we adjust drafts, get the smoke moving the right way again and open doors and windows to clear the air.

There have also been times when dissension over some matter, doctrinal or behavioural, threatens the loving unity of the little congregation. The discipline of the little church in the small village lies chiefly in this: there is no "better church" across the street. Knowing that rifts might take three generations to heal, and that if we splinter we will not survive, we "make every effort to keep the unity of the Spirit through the bond of peace" (Eph 4:3).

Like any church that is involved in ongoing evangelism, there is always the challenge of balancing preaching and teaching, of ensuring that we do not become an infantile church able to handle only the "elementary things" and never explore deeper into the word of God, problems warned against in Hebrews chapters 5 and 6.

So our little village church, cast-iron stove that it is, faithfully stoked and lovingly tended, goes on burning steadily, a source of warmth and light for a community. Once in a while, as we sit in our living room in front of our wood stove, we can watch a log suddenly catch fire as a lick of blue flame caresses it, or see tiny balls of gas explode into purest flame. These moments are exquisitely beautiful, like the moments when God calls a new person into life or when the church senses with awe the palpable presence of God.

The rest of the time it just burns on unspectacularly, steadily, patiently, casting its warm glow against the darkness and the cold.

20

TASTE AND SEE THAT THE LORD IS GOOD

The law of the Lord is perfect,
reviving the soul
The statutes of the the Lord are trustworthy
making wise the simple . . .
The ordinances of the Lord are sure
and altogether righteous . . .
they are sweeter than honey,
than honey from the comb.

PSALM 19:7–11

This Christmas I will pile the Christmas oranges in my new crystal bowl. The one I used all the previous years broke this past summer. Its hundreds of shimmering chunks and chips, scattered across my kitchen floor, shone iridescent through my tears. I do not usually mourn loss and breakage; I learned from my mother to gather up a broken glass or a shattered plate with a sigh, to say, "It's only a thing, after all."

But this crystal bowl was special, a wedding gift I had come to treasure more with each passing year. It had become a beloved link between my present stage of life and the early years of homemaking, child-rearing and starting out in farming, when the sun shining on its hundreds of beautifully cut facets cheered my heart on some very bleak midwinter days when either our tax payment or the latest baby was due. Or overdue.

So when the bowl fell, it represented more than just a "thing." It represented all the years it had made lovely by its silent, sun-catching presence. It represented moments of light amid greyness, a touch of luxury in the midst of hardship, friendships that sustained us. It represented my own gradual growth in understanding that beauty nurtures our spirits.

After the bowl broke, my children, by then all young adults, collaborated to replace it. When I felt the weight of the gift box, I knew immediately what was in it. But they, wisely, had not tried to replace it exactly. The new cut-glass bowl is very different from the one that broke; modern and clean in design, a clear-edged geometric instead of the baroque style of the bowl that broke, it represents my children's vision of the beautiful just as the bowl I broke represented our generation's. The new bowl, since then, has blessed special occasions in our family life just as the first crystal bowl blessed and connected such occasions for the first thirty-two years of our marriage.

The two bowls represent something else, too: the first was the gift of an older generation to a younger; the second was the gift of a younger generation to an older. I, at mid-life, am a grateful recipient of gifts from both generations.

I look at the new bowl scattering rainbows around itself and realize how my life has been blessed by the gifts of knowledge of and love for Scripture of a previous generation and by the honest struggle of my own young people and others whom I teach to be engaged in their culture while staying true to the gospel of Jesus Christ and his Word in the Scriptures.

I think of how a hermeneutic approach based on the notes in my father's beloved Scofield Bible sustained my earliest inquiries into Scripture and how a different, more historical and yet equally reverent hermeneutic now guides my study. I now recognize to a greater degree that the "true light which lights everyone who comes into the world" is refracted by the human act of writing and reading, the sun shining on and through the cut-glass bowls of human thought, but not thereby less true or less light.

This year, I will pile the Christmas oranges in the new, cleanly designed crystal bowl, but I will always remember with loving appreciation the earlier one. Likewise, I will always respect the intricacy of designs of interpretation by which the Book of Daniel and the Book of Revelation could be matched in richly detailed charts; even more I value typological readings of the tabernacle and the offerings which offered me "whole book" readings inherited from the earliest days of the Christian church.

I see a simpler plan now, by which the Bible is *both* sixty-six specific works directed in particular literary forms to specific historic audiences—*and* one great Book which, through the Spirit's enlightening of both writer and readers, still speaks God's truth to the church as a whole, and to me individually; arching rainbows of truth that trace the trajectory of God's grace through the whole drama of Creation, Fall, Redemption and Consummation.

Approached by different hermeneutic methods over time, the Scripture has been and continues to be sustaining of my spiritual and intellectual life. A senior English professor asked me one day how I came to know the Bible so well. When I told him it had been as much a staple as love and food in the family in which I grew up, read with our daily meals, talked about, taught and loved, he said in a quiet voice, full of unabashed envy, "What a wonderful heritage!"

I would like to pass to him—and to all I can reach—the shining crystal bowl, full of sweet, juicy Christmas oranges and to say, "O taste and see that the Lord is good."

LIFE:
A FIRST DRAFT ONLY

Reflections on Gifting and God's Process

21

LIFE: A FIRST DRAFT ONLY

And we, who with unveiled faces all reflect the Lord's glory, are being transformed into his likeness with ever-increasing glory, which comes from the Lord, who is the Spirit.

2 CORINTHIANS 3:18

The other day I was getting ready to mail one of those promo packages that people request from speakers—press photo, author biography, the bits and pieces of a person's life that brochures and posters and news releases are made of. Characteristically, I was in a hurry and was quickly pulling things from files to jam into an envelope. I turned the black-and-white photo over to stamp it with my name and address, reached into the jumble of my top desk drawer for a rubber stamp and pressed firmly. And there, on the back of my picture, the words "Draft Only" stared back at me. Startled, I laughed and then reached for the return address stamp I had meant to grab.

I later reflected that the stamp I had used first was peculiarly appropriate. For I am in the process of becoming—in a number of ways. In the novel *A Discovery of Strangers*, Rudy Wiebe writes of old people as "Those who Know Something a Little." It is a little frightening, now, to realize that I will either gain wisdom and pass it on or pass by wisdom and never achieve it. The danger of gaining knowledge without gaining its counterpart, wisdom, surely haunts any person who goes on learning. That holy fear of the Lord, which is the beginning of wisdom, grips me as I read Scripture or take a walk on a night bright with stars or washed with the Northern Lights. It is the beginning of wisdom, too, to know that when we have learned all we can, we still "know in part and...prophesy in part" (1 Cor 13:9).

My work as a writer, too, is hemmed in with finitude. I would not want a draft of my writing to be mistaken for my finished work. Stamping it "Draft Only" reminds both me and any reader that the work is still in process. Everyone who writes knows how ragged and rugged a first, second, and even a third draft is.

I think of writing a first draft as something akin to a potter clawing raw clay out of a hillside—there are so many stages of washing and wedging and shaping and firing that lie between that moment and a finished work. But a start must be made; the clay must be clawed out, the process begun.

It keeps me from despair to remember what I learned in one long dark night of soul-struggle soon after my first book was published. After a long illness, I lay in a hospital bed and felt that I was dying. One by one I brought the concerns of my life to God as arguments that I should go on living, and one by one I found myself compelled by a stern love to commit the loves of my life—husband, children, work—into God's hands.

With regard to my writing, I had a sudden illumination that told me that everything I write on this side of death, will from the perspective of the Other Side, look like a child's copybook, full of practice lines and blots; that even when I have done my very best, it is "Draft Only" for the work of praise that will be mine to write when I will "see the King in his beauty" (Isa 33:17).

All of life is a practice session for becoming the people we are meant to be. Despite the prevailing attitude in our society that we peak at age twenty-five or thirty-five or forty-five, with everything after that an anticlimax, a sort of long afterthought, the reality is that we are still only in draft until the final copy. Always and at every moment, we are only a first draft of our future selves. John writes, "Now we are the children of God, and what we will be has not yet been made known" (1 John 3:2). Writing to the believers at Ephesus, Paul reminds them that they were chosen in order "that in the coming ages [God] might show the incomparable riches of his grace" in and through them (Eph 2:7).

In "Weight of Glory," the title essay of a collection of addresses, C. S. Lewis expounds the wonder of what we are becoming and warns, "It is a serious thing to ... remember that ... the dullest and most uninteresting person you talk to may one day be a creature which, if you saw it now, you would be strongly tempted to worship ... There are no *ordinary* people."

Like you, I am a work in process, a piece of clay clawed by God's grace out of the riverbank—being washed, kneaded, wedged, placed on the potter's wheel, shaped by the pressure of God's hands and formed into a vessel "for noble purposes, made holy, useful to the Master" (2 Tim 2:21).

Or, to use the analogy I know much better as a writer, I am in "Draft Only." Revisions that amount to transformations keep going on as God continues to clarify the meaning and intent of my life.

Knowing this keeps me from undue discouragement and despair. When there are lines crossed out, plans changed, or life quite suddenly rearranged in ways I had not expected, I can believe that the Editor-in-Chief is doing the necessary polishing to make of me a work that will bring pleasure to the Craftsperson and praise to the Creator. One day, fully knowing and being fully known, I will better reflect my Creator's purpose.

Meanwhile, bear with me, as I with you. We are still stamped with finitude, fallibility and mortality. We are all still in "Draft Only."

22

SILENCED SERVANTS, SHOUTING STONES

"I tell you ... if they keep quiet, the stones will cry out."

LUKE 19:39–40

At the time of his Triumphal Entry into Jerusalem, Jesus declared that were his followers' praises to be hushed, the very stones along the roadside would shout out the silenced praises. I wonder what he would say today to the silencing of the voices of women in the church.

We have been given a place, of course. We can sing (even solos), be part of worship teams, "share" (most often with other women) and teach Sunday school. But in many evangelical churches women are still denied the opportunity to use teaching and preaching gifts within the worshipping congregation as a whole. A few difficult New Testament texts (1 Cor 14:34–35; 1 Tim 2:11–15) have been used to suppress the clear evidence that women in the early church did teach and preach, pray and prophesy (e.g., Acts 18:18–28 and 21:9; Rom 16:1, 2; 1 Cor 11:5), and to deflect the clear thrust of the gospel message toward the liberating of God's people from gender-determined roles into "the glorious liberty of the children of God" (Rom 8:21).

God's creatures must praise; they must use their gifts in his worship; and gifts must be called into the glad service of the risen Christ. When this does not happen, not only do the gift-bearers suffer, but the whole body is impoverished, for it fails to receive the gifts given for its life and work by the risen, exalted Lord.

Long ago, as I sought the Lord's blessing on my own sense of call into teaching the Word, God granted me emancipation from cultural bondage through the words Peter quoted in that great inaugural sermon of the church:

> In the last days, God says,
> I will pour out my Spirit on all people.
> Your sons *and your daughters* will prophesy…
> Even on my servants, *both men and women,*
> I will pour out my Spirit in those days,
> And they will prophesy. (Acts 2:17, 18)

I have added the emphasis as it was added to my own heart. I can still remember the rush of joy I felt as I realized that the church, God's covenant community of "the last days" operates under this great general promise. And it is to this general promise that any specific texts must be squared if we are to be true to the Lordship of Jesus Christ.

It is in Jesus' exaltation that the gift-giving Spirit is poured out on the church as we are told in Eph 4:7–13; and it is to his glory that all of the Spirit's gifts are to be gladly, joyfully and freely used by all believers. It is also the risen, exalted Lord of the church to whom we will render account for gifts denied, stifled, wrapped up and buried.

Despite my own personal assurance that these gifts and the mandate to use them are from the Holy Spirit, it took me much of my adult life to find biblical exposition to match the witness of the Spirit to my spirit. And so it was with fascination and delight that I read Richard Clark Kroeger and Catherine Clark Kroeger's *I Suffer Not a Woman: Rethinking 1 Timothy 2:11–15 in Light of Ancient Evidence* (Baker, 1992). The book is a model of historical scholarship, painstaking attention to the language of Scripture and sound hermeneutic practice.

My study and teaching of sixteenth- and seventeenth-century theological discussion has also made me realize how long the language of Scripture has been used to rob women of their voices within the church and how long it has taken us to hear the whole counsel of Scripture to set women free in service and worship. Almost like the Little Mermaid, who had to give up her voice in order to enter into love, women have been required to give up their voices in order to enter into the life of many evangelical churches.

Of course, we have found ways of speaking. It was while I was in a rural church under the leadership of a repressive male pastor that I first began to write. I was not allowed to preach in a church of thirty-five people, but I could write and be read internationally by any number of readers, even quoted from any number of pulpits. I was not being intentionally subversive, of course. Nonetheless, the fact that women have gone on writing and reading theological books—especially of the applied, practical kind—has given them a kind of voice denied the in the pulpit.

Another way that women have found voice in our churches has been through liturgical art. A glance at *Art of the Spirit* by Toronto writers Helen Bradfield, Joan Pringle and Judy Ridout (Dundurn Press, 1992) shows how these women fabric artists preach, teach and praise with needle and thimble, transforming silence into eloquent statements of truth and worship.

Even in churches where women are not allowed to speak, they have emblazoned their love for God and his people in banners under which the church meets, in cloths for the tables where we break bread together, in hangings for the pulpits from which the Word is spoken, in food spread on tables.

It is time for the church of Jesus Christ to re-awaken to the silenced gifts of gifted women and to cry out for forgiveness, not just to women, but to the great gift-giver himself for the denial of those gifts he has chosen to give. If everything that has breath, and even those elements without breath cry out his glory, then all the rocks of the Canadian shield and the great piles of the mighty Rockies would be shouting, clamouring on behalf of the too-long silenced voices of women in the church.

23

HOLDING UP THE MIRROR

*We have different gifts, according to the grace given to each
of us. If your gift is prophesying, then prophesy in accordance
with your faith. If it is serving, then serve; if it is teaching,
then teach; if it is to encourage, then give encouragement.*

ROMANS 12:6-8 (TNIV)

There is a brief scene in John Bunyan's *Pilgrim's Progress,
Second Part* where the new believers, Christiana and Mercy
come up from "the Bath Sanctification" (Bunyan's allegorical
depiction of baptism), each radiating a beauty that is quite
unearthly. But, Bunyan writes, "When the Women were thus
adorned they...could not see that glory each one on her self,
which they could see in each other."

The Christian ministry of encouragement is about seeing the
beauty of Christ in one another—and holding up a mirror so
that the other person can catch a glimpse of that beauty which
she cannot see in herself.

Sometimes encouragement simply means putting words
around what may seem obvious enough not to need mentioning.

"You are always there for me at just the right time," I tell a friend whose calls seem divinely ordered to meet my needs.

"I love it when you wear that jacket," a friend tells me. "You brighten our lives." I am encouraged to know that even what I choose to wear can make a difference.

Both partners in a marriage need to feed on words of honest encouragement. All of us can look around the circle of our friendships and our love and identify the gifts that others give us—and then put that acknowledgement into words, either voiced or in a card or note. (Or as one friend did for her husband, with a heart outlined in lipstick on the dresser mirror and the words, "You're looking at the most wonderful, handsome man in the world.") Words of loving encouragement translate into validation of the person.

Sometimes encouragement requires seeing something by faith that is not readily visible, either to the individual or to others. It requires seeing what God is about to do in that person's life, identifying a dimension of personality or character visible at that time only to the eyes of one who sees all the potential of God's power within that person and who loves the person towards a realization of that potential.

I once had a sudden and quite sure sense that a new believer I was nurturing in the faith had been or would be given a particular spiritual gift. I named it to her: "You may not be aware of it yet," I told her, "but I believe that God has given you the gift of evangelism and will use you to effectively share the gospel with many others." She looked at me, bewildered by what I was saying, her eyes clouded by depression. She could not see herself as I saw her, as I believed God saw her—complete in Christ, gifted for ministry—as others would come to see her in time.

I do not want to over-claim prophetic insight in giving this encouragement. Some of what I saw was based on my knowledge of the woman's natural gifts: her ability to relate to others, her sociability and personal grace, which made her a natural to "gossip the gospel." Some of it was a sense of her strategic social placement in the community: she was related by blood or marriage to most of the people in it.

But some of what I saw in her was glimpsed by revelation. I saw—for a moment or two—something of the glory of what God was doing and would do in her life. Over the next years, my friend did indeed become a key person in leading people to faith in Jesus Christ. My part had been to see what God was about in this woman's life, to prepare and equip her for her ministry and to encourage her to move in the direction of using her gifts.

"Thank you for the note you left me," a woman wrote to me recently from New Zealand, where she had ministered to me as my speaker caregiver at a couple of weekend conferences. "I don't quite see myself as you do, but what you said is what I long to be for Christ." That's what encouragement is all about: holding up a mirror so another can see, more and more, that the loveliness of Christ is showing through.

24

MAPPING THE SPIRITUAL EXPERIENCE

Posterity will serve him; future generations will be told about the Lord. They will proclaim his righteousness to a people yet unborn—for he has done it.

PSALM 22:30-31

I am looking at a world map dated 1670, a fascinating record of the world as it was perceived following the early voyages of discovery. Its inaccuracies are as interesting as its accuracies.

As a Canadian, the blank space left along the northwest coast of North America is particularly interesting. An accurate map of that area could not yet be drawn; the mapmaker, Frederick de Wit, simply acknowledged the incompleteness of human knowledge by leaving the coastline unfinished.

Maps fascinate me—not only the maps of geographers, but also the maps of experience left by storytellers. Izaak Walton, for instance, writing in the seventeenth century, mapped out the lives of several great spiritual statesmen of his era and the one preceding, describing their personalities and the way of God's grace in their lives. Walton also gracefully describes his affection for fishing and leaves us a map of his own deeply quiet Christlikeness in *The Compleat Angler* (1653). In the introspective writings of Sir Thomas Browne, a seventeenth-century doctor, we see committed belief confronting the challenge of skepticism at the very dawn of the modern era.

Out of the welter of map-making in the 1600s arose the greatest story-map of all time, *The Pilgrim's Progress,* mapping the Christian life in such precise and memorably etched scenes that even now, more than three hundred years since Bunyan wrote, most people still know something about the Slough of Despond or Vanity Fair or Doubting Castle.

Life, like the voyages of discovery, is infinitely complex and variable. Yet certain routes and particular stages can be identified as nearly universally experienced. For this reason, maps in the form of stories about other people's lives or in the form of guides to stages continue to fascinate us. And map-making by means of narratives of experience continues to be an avenue by which we can effectively describe the Christian experience to our culture.

The only problem is that the twentieth-century maps made by evangelical Christians have often been woefully deficient in both honesty and artistry. We have mapped the Christian life as lived in two simple stages: before conversion—with everything dark and chaotic—and after conversion—with everything bathed in pink light and suffused with a sort of misty loveliness.

But Bunyan had it right. Conversion itself is a very long process of hearing and responding to the call of God, of slipping into despair, of seeking easier alternatives to the absolute commitment that entry at the "little wicket gate" actually calls for.

Justification, the action of God in response to our recognition of Christ's death having been *for us,* is instantaneous—as the Reformers rightly insisted. This is depicted in *The Pilgrim's Progress* as the exchange of the Pilgrim's rags for a "Broidered

Coat" of Christ's righteousness to be worn for the rest of his journey.

But sanctification, the process by which we become holy, is a lifelong process, with its Valleys of Humiliation, face-to-face encounters with the evil Apollyon and, most frightening of all, its "Inchanted" Ground, where some pilgrims simply fall asleep and so never complete the journey. But it also has its House Beautiful, the fellowship of believers, and its Delectable Mountains, where the things of God are more clearly understood and found to be sweet and refreshing, and its Beulah Land, the stage of maturity into which God's people can enter when the great battles of life—except for that final one, with Death—have been fought.

How shall we create maps for our lost and confused generation? By telling our stories—our own stories and the stories of others who have made trails before us or alongside us; by being honest about the hard places as well as the glorious final destination; by leaving blanks to indicate that some things are just not yet known. Our maps, too, will have their idiosyncrasies, inaccuracies and incompleteness for future generations to chuckle over, to correct, to extend. But they will demonstrate that life has shape, meaning, value and, above all, destination.

There are, of course, writers and communicators who have done this superbly: C. S. Lewis tells the story of his conversion in *Surprised by Joy*; Frederick Buechner writes movingly of his faith in *The Sacred Journey*; Emilie Griffin tells her story in *Turning: Reflections on the Experience of Conversion*.

Canadian mapmakers of the experience of conversion and the life that follows have also added their story-maps to mainstream culture. The artist William Kurelek writes of walking out of depression into the light of salvation in his autobiography,

Someone With Me; Margaret Avison describes the in-breaking of light after knowing only "winter sun" in her collection, *The Dumbfounding*; Rudy Wiebe's pioneering work in writing fiction out of the Mennonite experience is being augmented by a chorus of excellent writers from that community.

But we need so many more mapmakers, people who can tell their stories without religious jargon and with transparent honesty in all of the forms of storytelling: song, poetry, fiction, biography and autobiography. In an age when people have pretty much tuned out sermons, storytellers are still heard.

In the great overthrow of the ancient serpent depicted in the Revelation, the means of victory is two-fold: "They conquered him by the blood of the Lamb and by the word of their testimony" (12:11). Jesus has done his part in this great conquest; we need to encourage one another to go on doing ours.

25

ON THE CARE AND
FEEDING OF BOOKWORMS

The fear of the LORD is the beginning of knowledge, but fools despise wisdom and discipline.

PROVERBS 1:7

Looking carefully at the tiny leather-bound volume I was returning to the librarian at the university's special collections library, I found myself wondering—as I often do with such old and rare books—about others who had read the book before me, about the community I was joining as I carefully turned its brittle pages. But then I saw that humans had not been the only audience for the book—a series of tiny holes in the edge of the leather cover told me that bookworms had been busy, too.

Bookworms! I have never actually *seen* one (although all my life I have been one), but I have often seen evidence of their drilling. Bookworms: silently, industriously at it somewhere, even as I write. And the human bookworms are at it, too—the scholars who pull books off the shelf and copy lines and sources and go on thinking and reconfiguring the store of human ideas.

What good are they—these scribbling "clerks" with glasses that thicken as they grow older? How do they fit into our busy world, where the chief work seems to be that of buying and selling? Are they just relics of a bygone age, or are they a form of life necessary to us all?

And how do Christian scholars contribute to the life of the church—when the really important things seem to be finding enough people to sit on committees, to run programs, to reach people with a direct proclamation of the gospel?

In short, is scholarship—by which I mean a steady committed engagement with a particular field of knowledge with the goal of transmitting it, illuminating it and adding to it—a waste of time that could be spent more profitably in other occupations? How does scholarship relate to the great commission?

As I have talked with young people engaged in graduate study, I have realized that these question are far more than academic: finding answers is of utmost importance if anyone is to continue studying with any sense that scholarship is an expression of faith and worship.

For many Christian graduate students, there is a "double whammy" in that they have to battle the attitude in the business community—often represented by loving parents who may be helping them financially—that what they are doing may not result in a secure job or add dollars to the economy; and they also have to face a lack of understanding within the church both of what they are studying and its possible significance to the Christian community.

Thankfully, the anti-intellectualism of the evangelical movement in North America has faded. Under the influence of such leaders as Carl Henry, Harold Ockenga and J. I. Packer, as well as a whole circle of Christian Reformed scholars, there has been a growing sense of the importance of thinking Christianly in every field of thought and life.

Sadly, however, some of the long-term results of a failure to engage in scholarship are still with us. There is a widespread lack of understanding and recognition for those who study beyond the level of job preparation.

So what if the person sitting down the row from you in church is doing a PhD dissertation in chaos theory or glaciation patterns or philosophy? The church will respectfully call that person "Doctor" when the program of studies is finally over, but who will have sat down and really asked about his or her work? Who will have really have cared for the particular kind of intellectual pain that the person may be bearing, the pain of having to live with an incomplete synthesis of faith and knowledge? Who will really have prayed for someone whose whole concept of reality is being defined against enormous challenges? Who will have valued the young scholar's work and helped him or her envision how his or her gifts could be used for worshipful service to our Lord and his kingdom?

I know far too many intelligent young scholars, who have studied at evangelical Bible schools or Christian liberal arts colleges, who now affirm no Christian beliefs. The typical attitude of the evangelical church has been to blame the university for this loss of faith. But perhaps at least part of the responsibility for the high numbers of young people who were raised within the faith and now are engaging in scholarship outside of it lies with the church itself, in its failure to recognize that scholars are—as Margaret Avison once said to me—the earthworms who toil away out of sight and underground to silently till and aerate the soil out of which all ideas grow.

The church has often failed to provide prayerful and personal support to those who are called into intellectual inquiry, failed to help developing scholars "hold fast those things delivered to them" even while engaging new ideas and challenges.

The price we have paid for our failure to nurture bookworms is high: we have sent out companies of missionaries who have learned how to communicate the gospel cross-culturally, but we have failed to develop people who can interpret and influence our own culture, to understand the prevailing ideas at their source in philosophy, and to contribute to the ongoing conversation that is scholarship in a tone of Christian understanding and commitment.

We need to encourage, feed and nurture bookworms—to affirm the significance of their unseen work, to share their struggles and to feed their spirits so that they, in turn, may help to equip the church to engage and challenge our culture in the years ahead.

26

ALL THE LITTLE BIRDS

My soul yearns, even faints, for the courts of the LORD; my heart and my flesh cry out for the living God. Even the sparrow has found a home, and the swallow a nest for herself, where she may have her young—a place near your altar, O LORD Almighty, my King and my God. Blessed are those who dwell in your house; they are ever praising you.

PSALM 84:2-4

Every spring, at the farm, the little birds come to our "window trees"—the Manitoba maple, chokecherry and ash that crowd around our country home. Suddenly appearing in the nearly leafless trees will be olive-cheeked warblers, thrushes, redpolls and those lovely rosy finches misnamed "purple"—all the little birds I love and welcome when they stop for a day or two, spring or fall, on their way to nest or to migrate for winter.

With the farm located under a flyway, we see big birds, too, on the their migratory journeys: the sandhill cranes with their undulating call, whooping cranes, trumpeter swans, Arctic geese, a flotilla of white pelicans and, of course, skein after skein of Canada geese.

Thrilling as the great birds are to see, it is the little birds I love, shyly coming up to present their modest colours, joining the small birds that stay for the summer. The pale yellow of warblers, the sudden gold of black-barred goldfinches, the barely glimpsed shimmer of green hummingbirds and the brown busyness of tilt-tailed wrens delight me more in their busy domesticity than do the circling, screaming hawks or even the silent herons, suddenly lifting from the river valley with slow dignity, pressing the twilight back with their great wings.

Because I love the little birds, I was delighted to find a phrase about them in the story of the Genesis flood. Every once in a while I enjoy reading the Bible in French—both to refresh myself in a language I love but seldom get to use and to gain the value of disorientation in reading familiar passages.

Our more prosaic English text tells us that Noah took with him "every bird according to its kind, everything with wings." But the French translation by Louis Segond adds a lovely turn of phrase. Noah took along with him *tous les petits oiseaux*: all the little birds!

Suddenly a lovely image comes to my mind—a cross between Noah-and-the-Ark scenes from Sunday school papers or flannel graph sets and pictures of St. Francis of Assisi. The image is of old, white-beared Noah with a wonderful flutter of small birds all around him.

The big birds—the eagles and herons, the vultures and ravens, the pelicans—have gotten aboard the ark on their own. It is the little birds that Noah has to gather up and take on board. Oh, the little birds: parakeets and hummingbirds, robins and thrushes, the chatty, brown wrens that scold in our trees and the blue-and-black "fairy wrens" we saw once in Tasmania.

On that trip, we were visiting with author Barney Roberts and his wife in their writing retreat when Barney invited us to watch him feed the wrens. He opened the front door to the morning sunshine and, tossing a few crumbs, began quietly talking, calling, crooning to the blue wrens. At first a shy little hen and then a brighter and bolder cock moved in from the bushes around the house to peck at the crumbs. Barney kept moving deeper back into the doorway, then finally right into the house, the small wrens following the trail of crumbs he was making for them, quite unafraid. Maybe that's how Noah got the little birds onto the ark.

What I love about the biblical phrase in French is the early reminder of what Jesus later taught very explicitly: that God has special providential care for the little things of his creation. Throughout Scripture, the little birds have a special place: the sparrow nesting on the altar (Ps 84:3), the sparrow whose fall is noted by a loving Father (Matt 10:29). Jesus gently jokes, Don't be afraid. You are more valuable than many sparrows. Than how many? Does it matter?

For those of us who join in with the little birds—fleeting, flitting, singing, chatting, seen briefly and gone, but each one "beautiful in its time" (Eccl 3:11), each an object—and object lesson—of God's tender care over every minute detail of his intricately designed creation—the phrase *tous les petits oiseaux* brings its own special joy and comfort. The little birds, too, were taken on the ark. They are part of the chorus of praise, part of the picture of God's saving mercy.

It helps those of us who know we do not qualify as "big birds" to be aware that God has a special interest in the "little birds." It helps me remember when the doorbell rings and a child presents a project or a scraped knee or a need for a cookie, or when a phone call interrupts my morning's work that God's care is for *tous les petits oiseaux*.

As children, we used to sing,

God sees the little sparrow fall
It meets his tender view
If God so loves the little things
I know he loves me too.

We were snug then, in our smallness, aware of a care that does not overlook the little ones. We can be snug, still, in that care.

ARTABAN'S DILEMMA

When [the Magi] had heard the king, they went on their way, and the star they had seen in the east went ahead of them. . . . When they saw the star, they were overjoyed!

MATTHEW 2:9–10

At the end of Henry Van Dyke's classic tale, *The Story of the Other Wise Man*, the fictitious fourth wise man named Artaban faces a decisive moment. After many interruptions in his search for the King, he must decide whether to keep his last treasure to offer to the one about to be crucified or use it to purchase the freedom of a weeping slave girl. "Was it his great opportunity or his last temptation? He could not tell."

For many of us, Artaban's dilemma is a daily one. We often have to make choices, and we do not always know whether we are facing an opportunity or a temptation. For me, the dilemma is nearly continuous. Opportunities to serve the larger community or the body as a whole present themselves along with the needs of family, neighbours and service in the local body of believers.

Often it is only in the doing that I have learned whether I have responded to an opportunity or succumbed to a temptation.

When there is joy, a sense that my gifts are being used for the kingdom, quiet peace, a deep inner sense of "yes," I know I have responded to opportunity. But when there is confusion in my mind and disturbance in my spirit, and I go home soul-weary and spent, I wonder if perhaps I have merely acquiesced to pressure, merely given in to the various temptations of a more public life or the wish to please those who call on me.

So what have I learned so far about distinguishing between "opportunity" and "temptation"? What criteria guide me as I seek to choose opportunity and to resist temptation? Here are some the questions I am learning to ask.

Is this my job or someone else's? Increasingly I am aware that if I take on too much, I rob others of opportunity that should be theirs. This became clear to me recently at one conference when the organizers asked me to take an extra session. I overcame my usual impulse to say, "Sure," and explained that I would not have the energy to do a fourth session.

When the conference came, the committee had filled the extra programme slot with a heart-quieting concert of classical music by two talented young women. My "no" had opened up a ministry opportunity to two other women—and had greatly enriched the day.

Can someone else do it? Many of the things we overload ourselves with could be done more capably by someone else. If a task is not using the unique configuration of gifts and abilities God has entrusted to me, it may be better to let someone else do it. For me this has meant saying "no" to various invitations to do tasks which may be important and worthwhile in themselves, but are tasks that I must leave for others more gifted.

Is it compatible with my central commitments? My commitment to love God with my whole self, heart, mind and strength is given practical expression in what Francis Bacon, a seventeenth-century essayist, calls "the discipline of humanity" that marriage and family life afford. Although Cam has been immensely supportive of me using my gifts of teaching and speaking for the good of the body as a whole, I keep fully and continuously accountable within our marriage. Sometimes a period of being "out there" is followed by a time of saying "no" to others and "yes" to needs within our own family and community.

What is the potential for clearly proclaiming the good news concerning Jesus Christ or equipping others for this great task? This is often difficult to assess, since God's wonderful, upside-down kingdom is often built in hidden and invisible ways. What may look like a "great opportunity" may be a time and energy waster—a temptation, in fact. It may—at a particular time—be more important to be present for my granddaughters than at the largest conference. Here I need to feel the gentle pressure of the Spirit towards accepting an invitation or turning it down—and to feel that pressure, I need to keep a place of stillness at the centre.

Do I experience joy as I do the task? Joy seeps up through nerves and tiredness, wells up past pressure and anxiety when the work I undertake is the work God has equipped and called me to do.

As we seek to hear and respond to God's call on our lives, we may not always get it right, but sometimes we will. On those occasions we will know something of Artaban's "calm radiance of wonder and joy." And at the end of our journey, we will have the assurance that the treasures we have expended to meet the needs of others, whether in hidden places or along the thoroughfares, are accepted as gifts offered to the King himself.